Star Bright
and the
Looking Glass

STAR BRIGHT
AND THE LOOKING GLASS

WRITTEN AND ILLUSTRATED BY

JONATHAN LUNA

IMAGE COMICS

IMAGE COMICS, INC.

www.imagecomics.com
www.lunabrothers.com
www.jonathanluna.com

Book design by Jonathan Luna
Title logo design by Jonathan Luna and Giancarlo Yerkes

STAR BRIGHT AND THE LOOKING GLASS
ISBN: 978-1-60706-600-2
First printing, November 2012

For international licensing inquiries, please write to: foreignlicensing@imagecomics.com

Printed in Korea

Special thanks to:

Andrea Goto

Aleem Hossain

Tim Ingle

Jenn Kao

Joshua Luna

Dan dos Santos

Meg Swecker

Sarah Vaughn

Kimberly Weigend

Samantha Winslow

Giancarlo Yerkes

ONCE UPON A TIME, there was a baby girl who was abandoned in the wood. Three young animals—Toad, Owl, and Capybara—found her in a clearing one night. Under the light of a full moon, the animals thought she looked like a bright star. And so they called her "Star Bright."

Together, the four grew up in the wood.

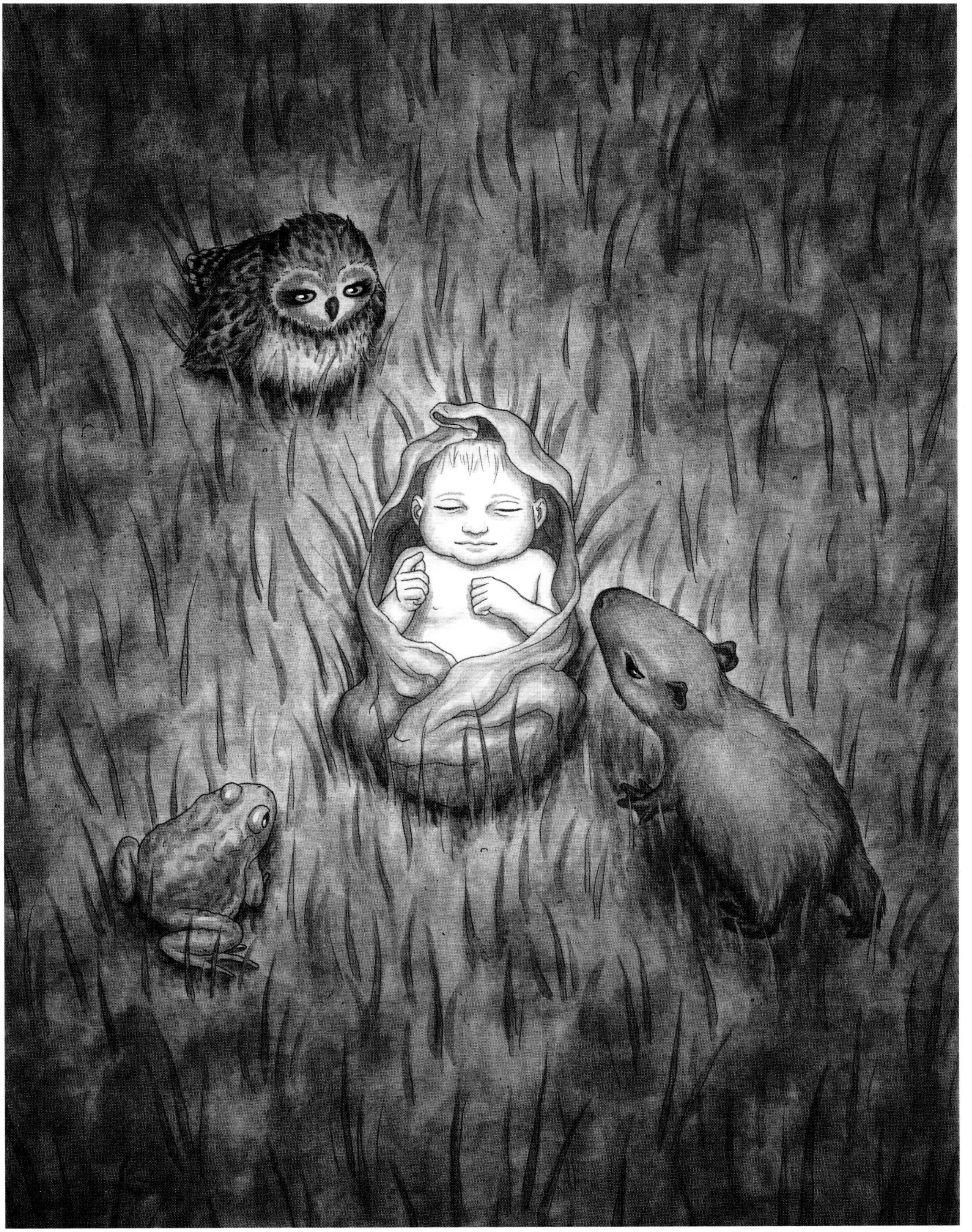

Star Bright spent her days lying about, picking flowers, and playing with her friends, Toad, Owl, and Capybara.

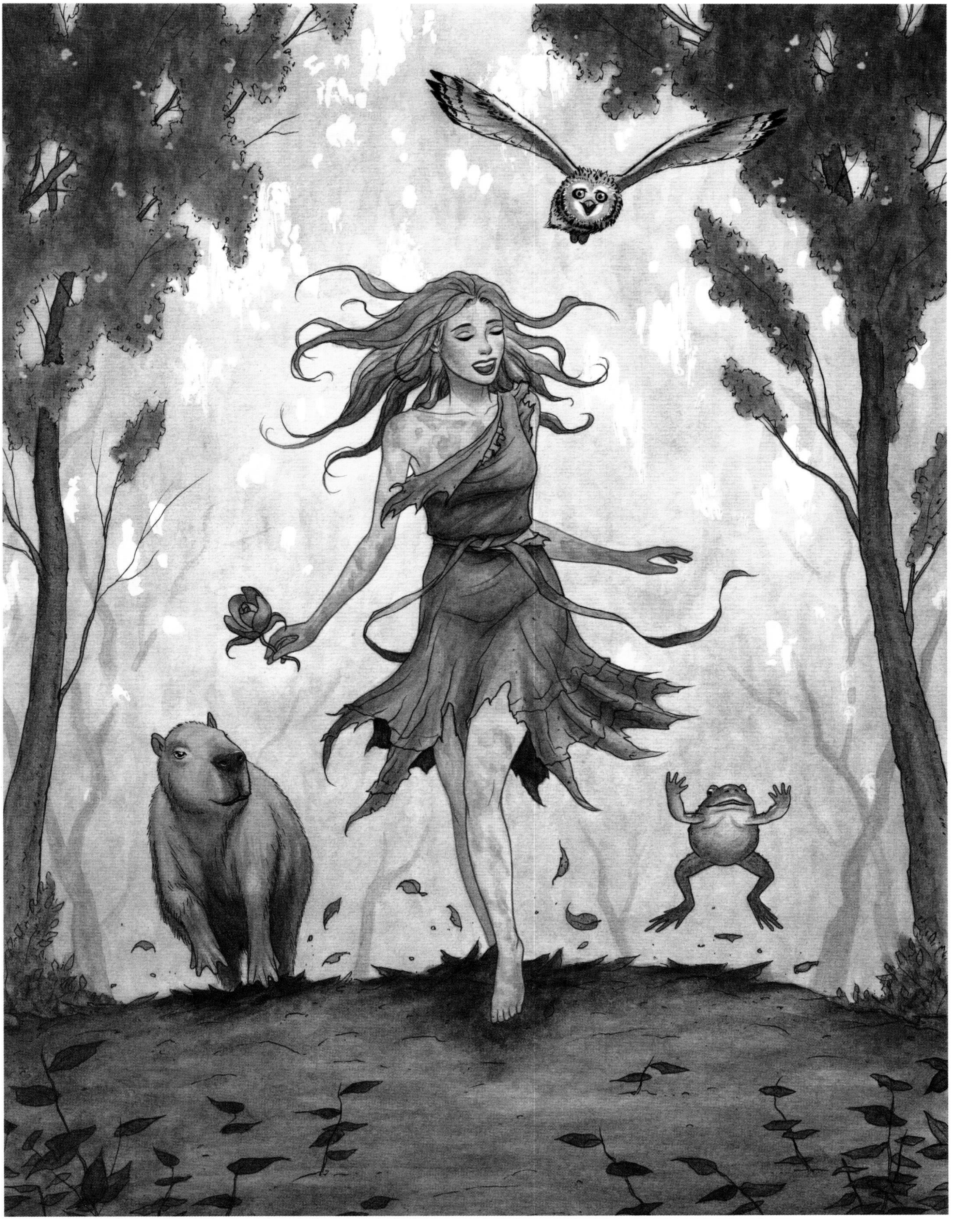

She was naturally beautiful, but quite dirty and unkempt. Her face was covered in layers of greasy grime collected over the years. Her hair was a tangled mess, often spattered with dirt and crawling with bugs. Her dress, traded from a passing merchant years before, was tattered and filthy.

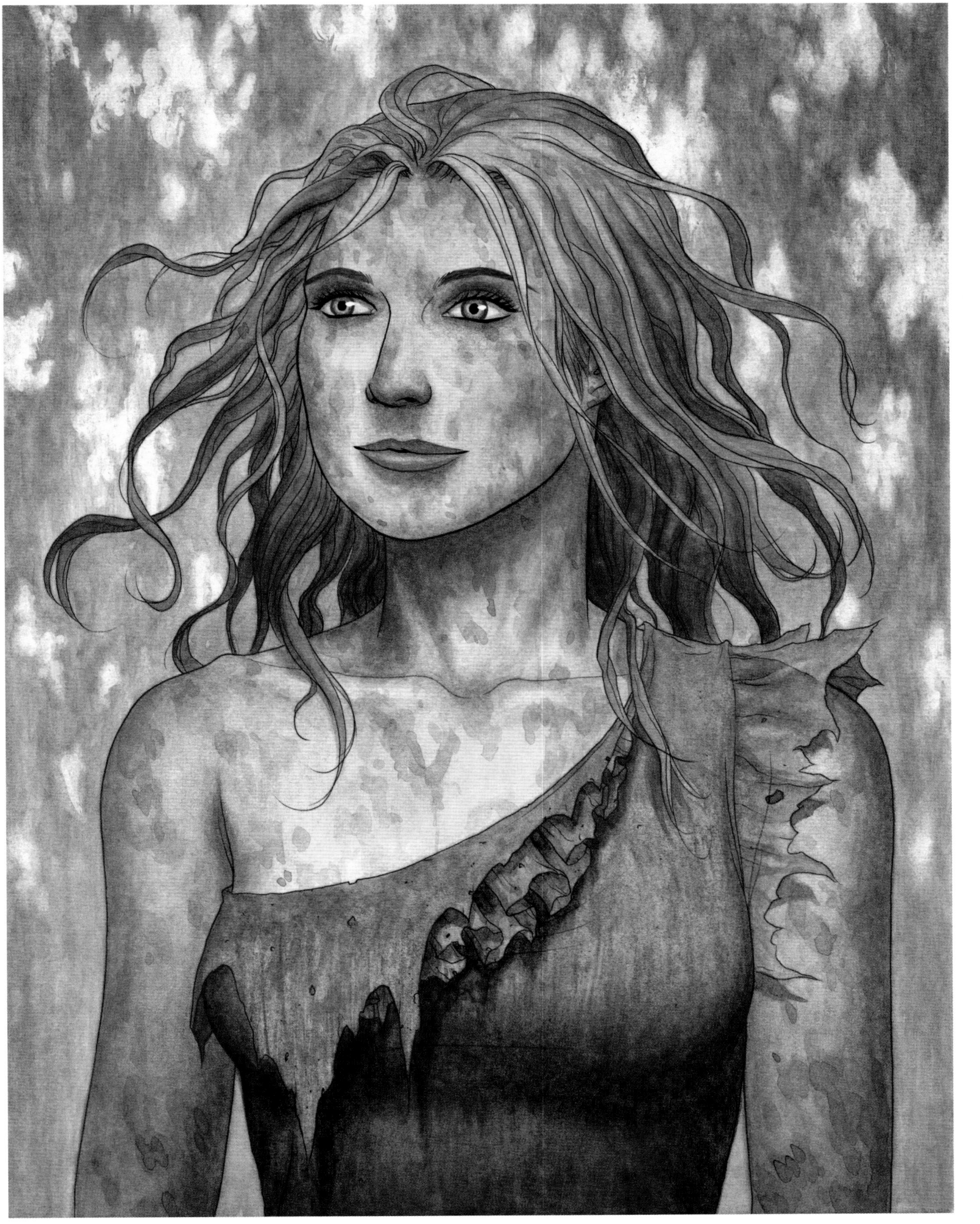

One day, while taking a stroll along her favorite pond with her friends, Star Bright found a strange object stuck in the ground.

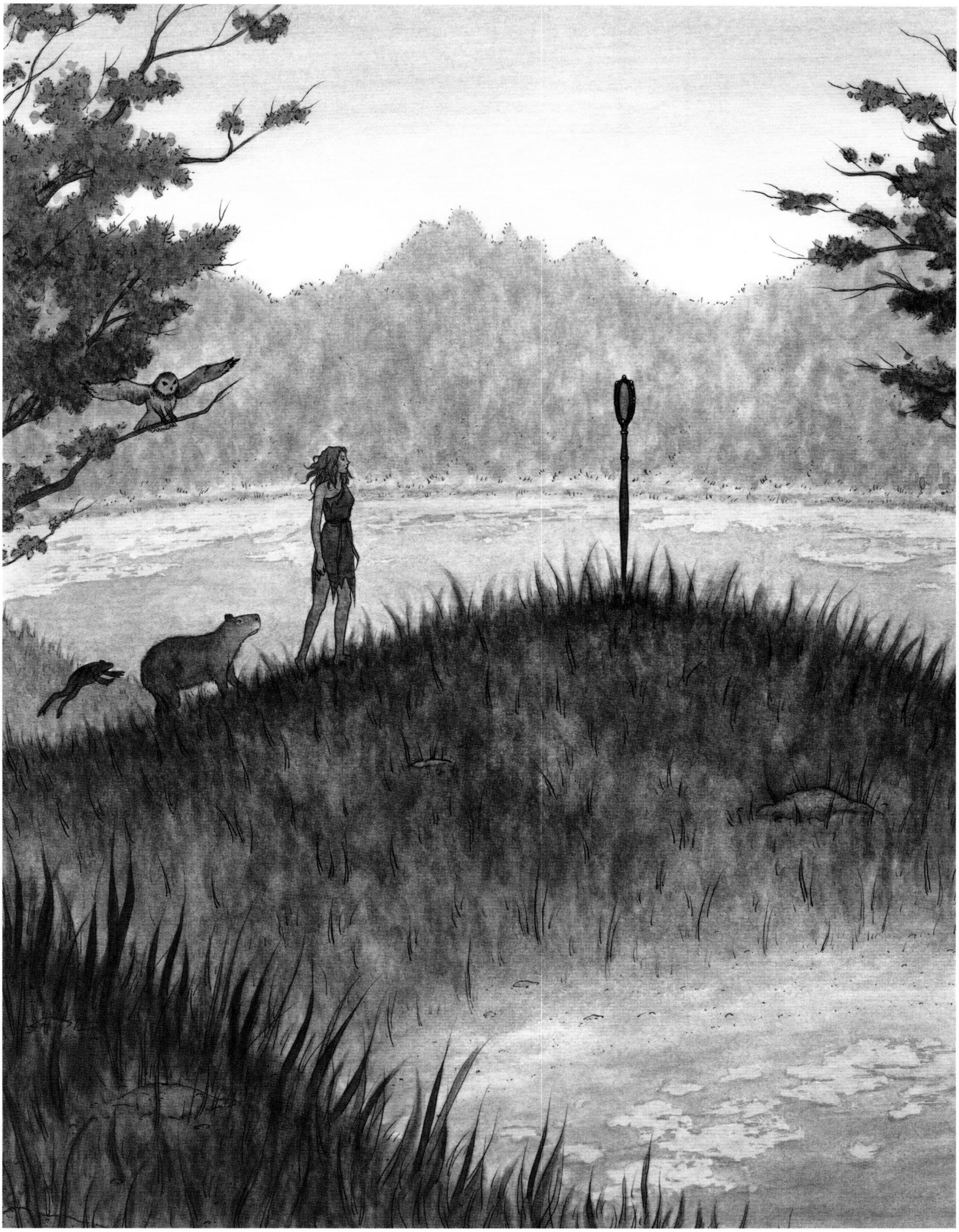

It was dark, shiny, ornate, and had a long staff for a handle. Nothing like it existed in the wood. Star Bright feared the object and kept her distance from it, but she was intrigued as well. Her curiosity was piqued.

"What is that?" she asked her friends, not turning away from the tall, mysterious thing.

The animals looked at each other and shrugged.

Owl said, "We have no idea, Star Bright. We've never seen anything like it before."

Walking up to the object, Star Bright saw herself in the shiny oval. She was startled. Certainly she had seen her own reflection in water before, but never as clearly as this.

Star Bright asked, "Is this...me? Is this what I look like?"

Taking a closer look at herself, she gasped.

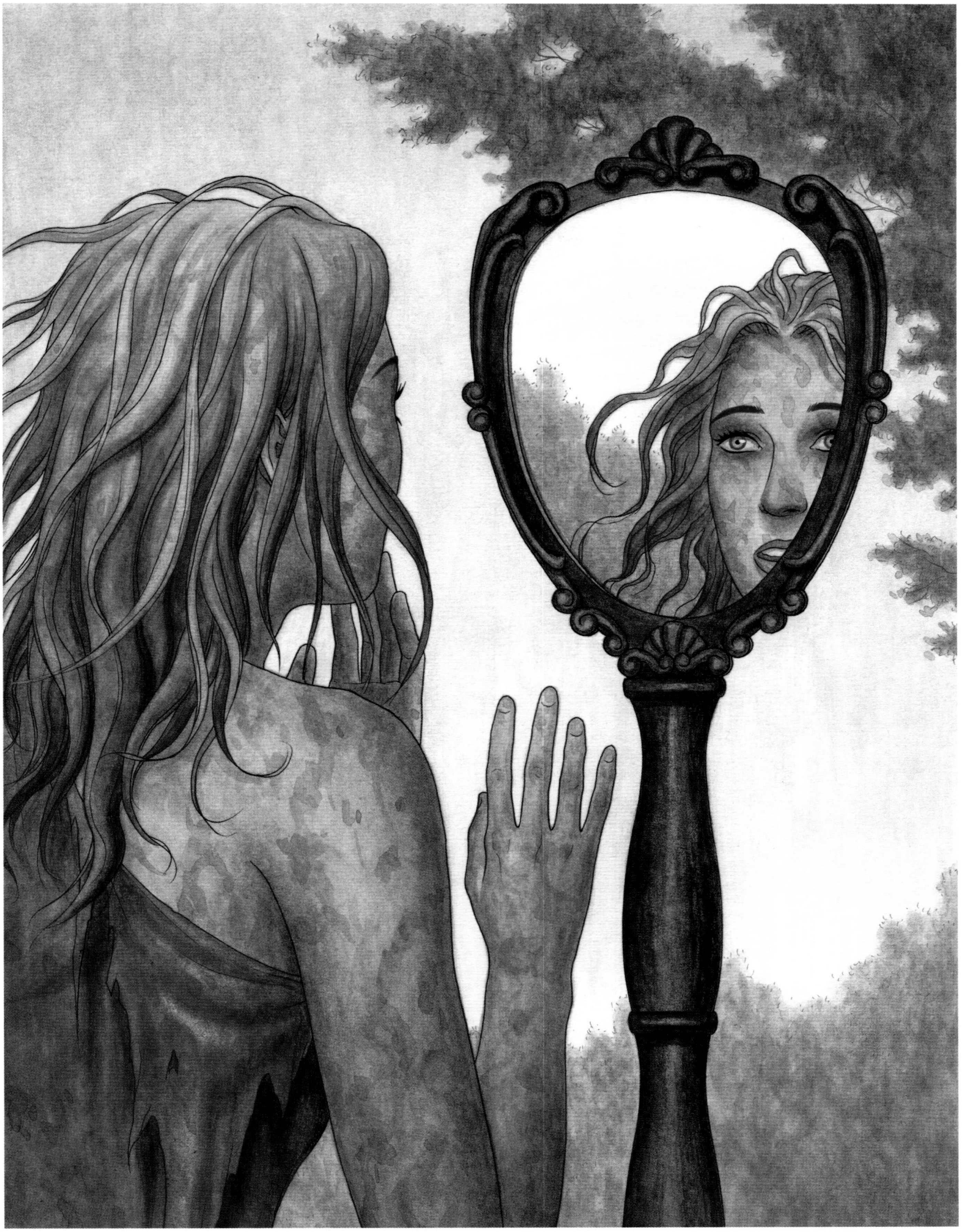

Star Bright turned to her friends and exclaimed, "I'm hideous! I had no idea I was this filthy and scruffy! Why hasn't anyone told me? Dear Toad? Dear Owl? Dear Capybara?"

The animals looked at each other again, confused.

"But, Star Bright...this is the way you've always looked to us," said Toad.

"We never thought you looked hideous," added Capybara.

"You've seen travelers come through the wood," said Star Bright. "You must've seen that I look disgusting by comparison."

The animals shrugged.

Star Bright began to inspect the object. "This shiny part is reflective like water," she said, then squinted. "Why isn't it wet? Why isn't it rippling or pouring out? Why can't I put my fingers through it?"

Star Bright didn't know what the object was called. She thought it looked like a combination of a cooking pan and a stick, so she decided to call it a "pan-stick."

She pulled the pan-stick out of the ground and kept it for herself.

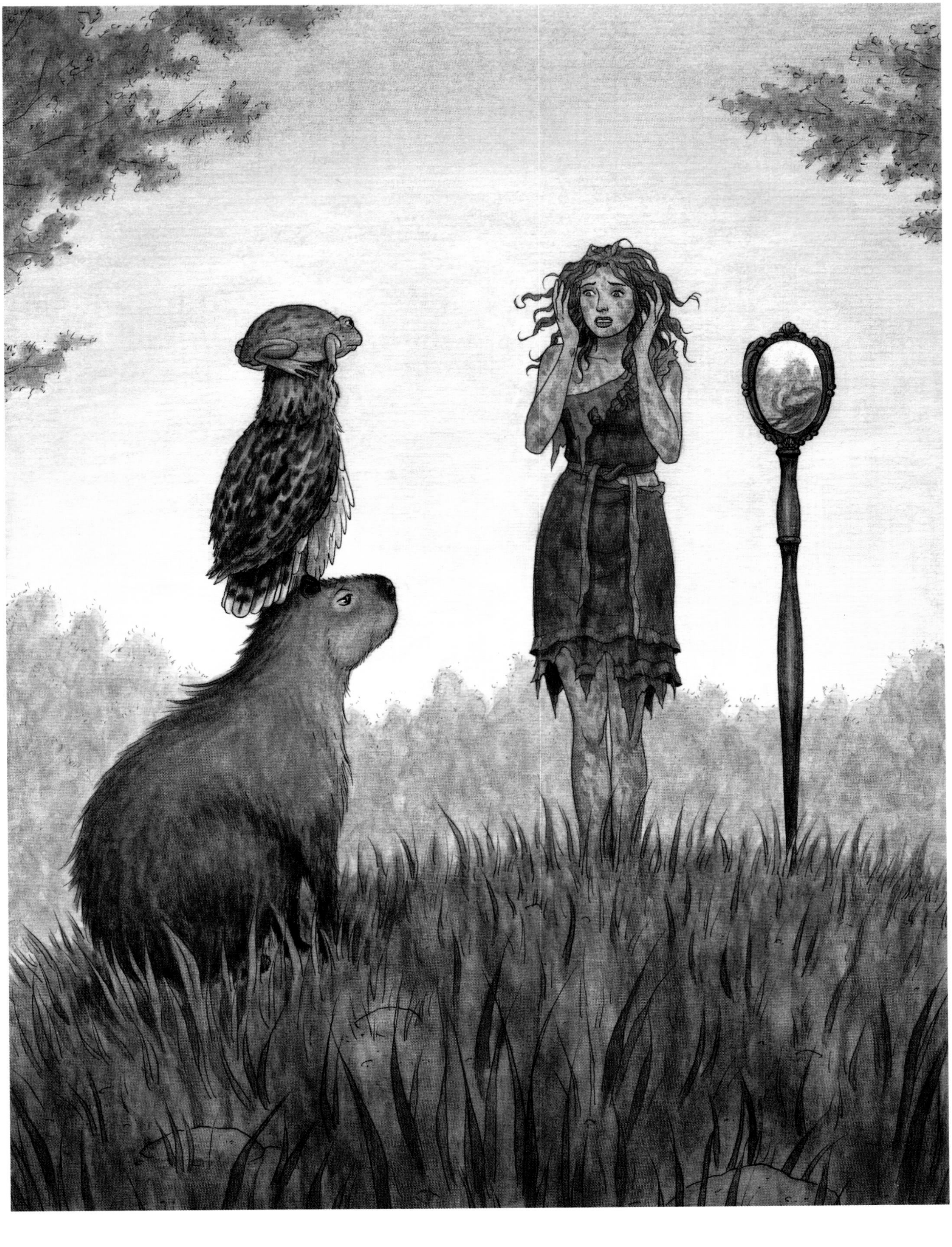

Star Bright began to work on her appearance. She spied on beautiful women who traveled with passing merchants, and wanted to emulate them.

First, she bathed in the pond. She had done so before, but this time she scrubbed for hours until she saw her reflection change in the pan-stick. The grime that had collected on her skin over the years was finally washed away. Her dress was once again white. Her hair was more golden than she could ever remember it being. Fish scattered from the cloud of dirt she created in the water.

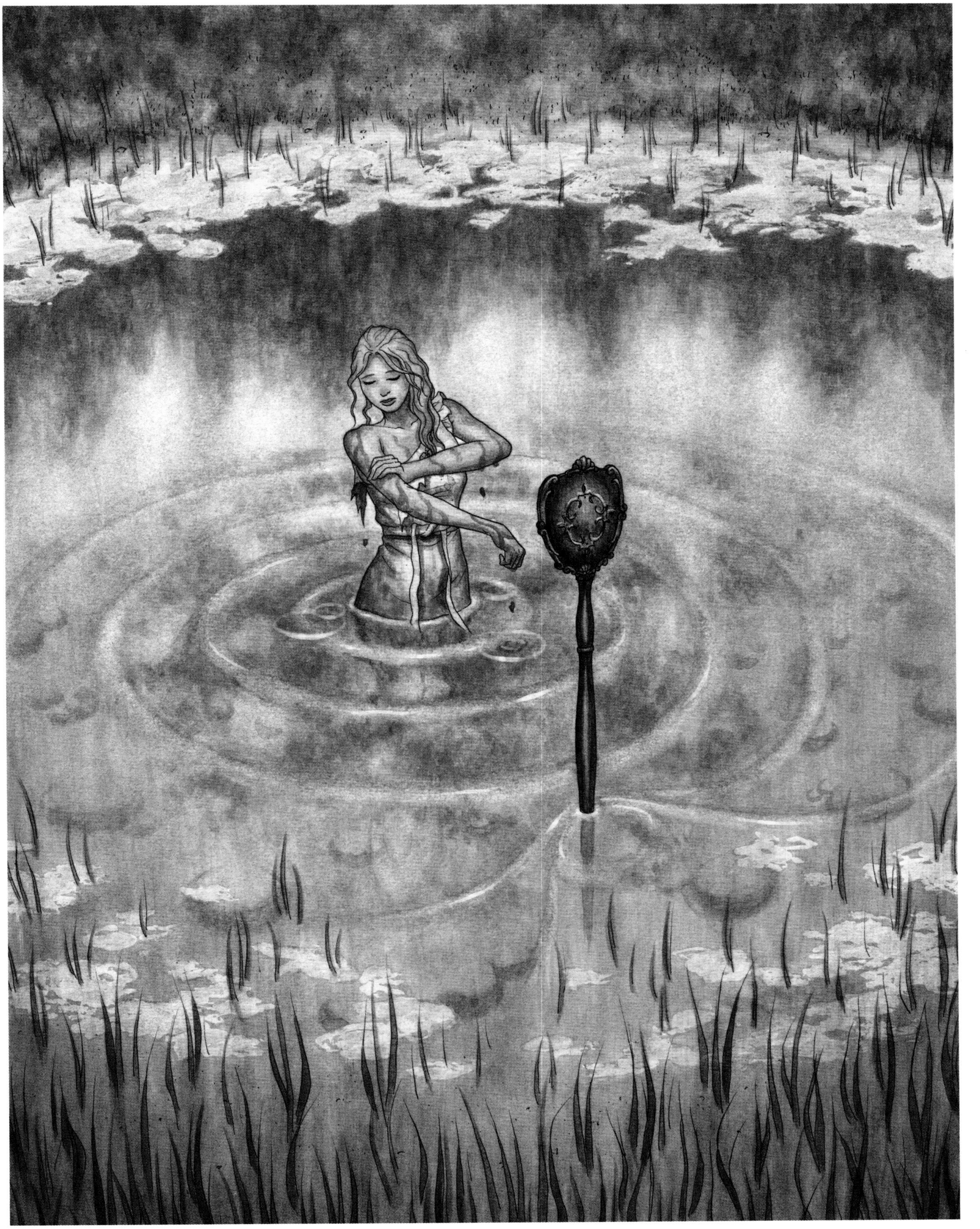

Second, she made a hairbrush by wrapping a piece of boar fur around a stick. Brushing her hair with the stiff boar bristles, she flung the dirt and bugs out. Her hair was now soft and wavy, instead of a tangled mess.

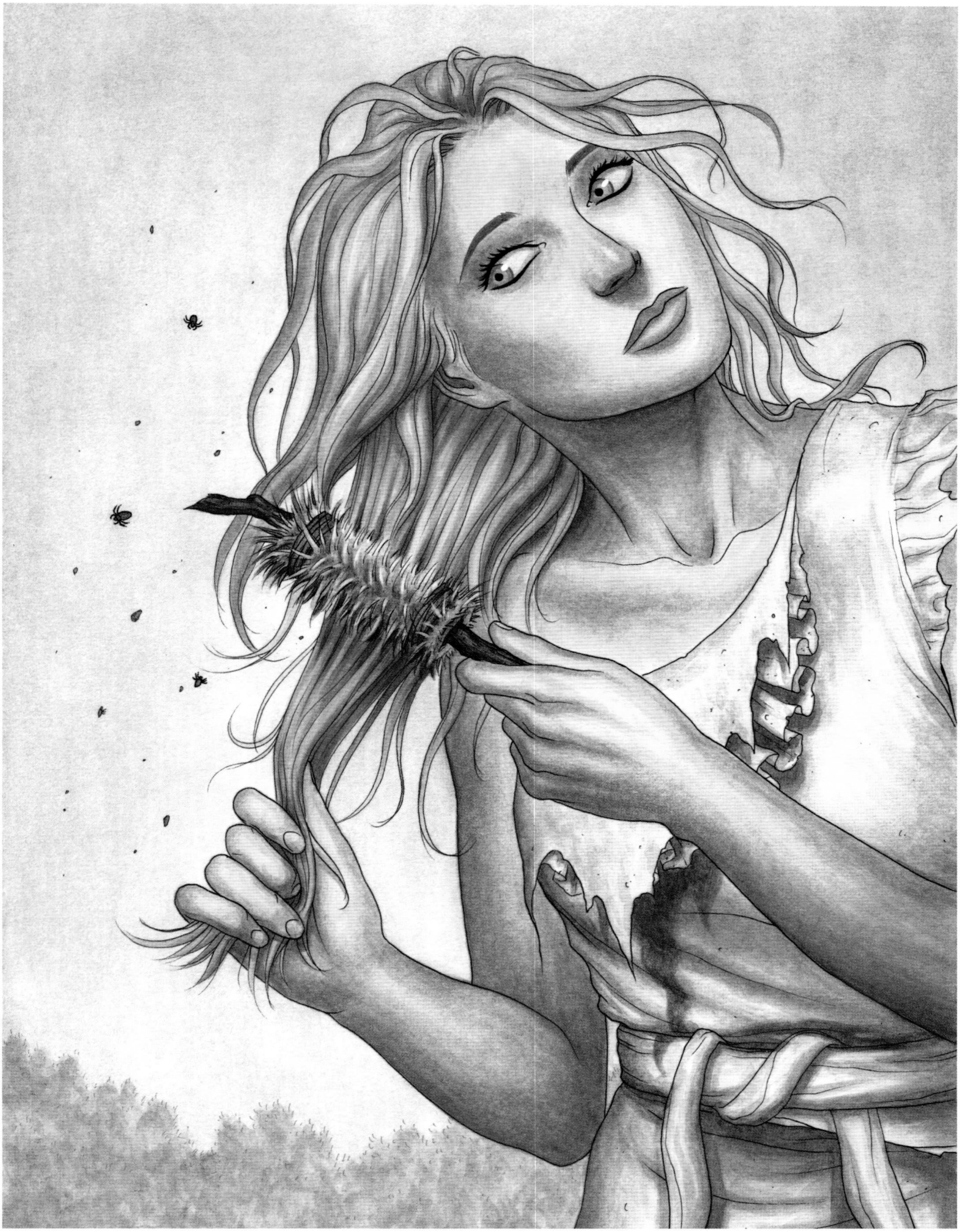

Then she mended her tattered dress with a needle and thread made from bone and flax.

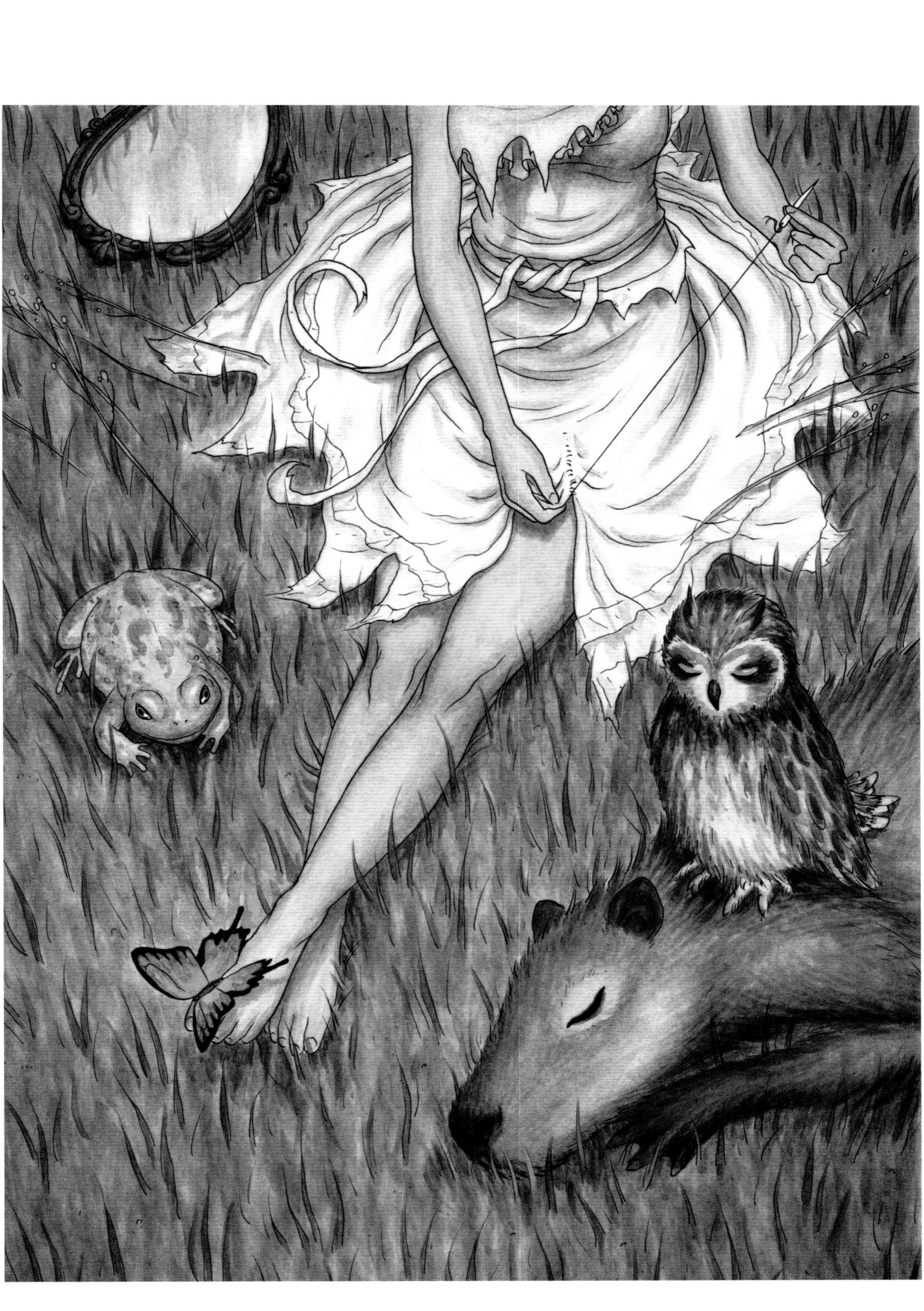

She even used pulverized chalk to smooth out her complexion and crushed mulberries to give redness to her cheeks and lips. To top everything off, she crowned herself with white roses.

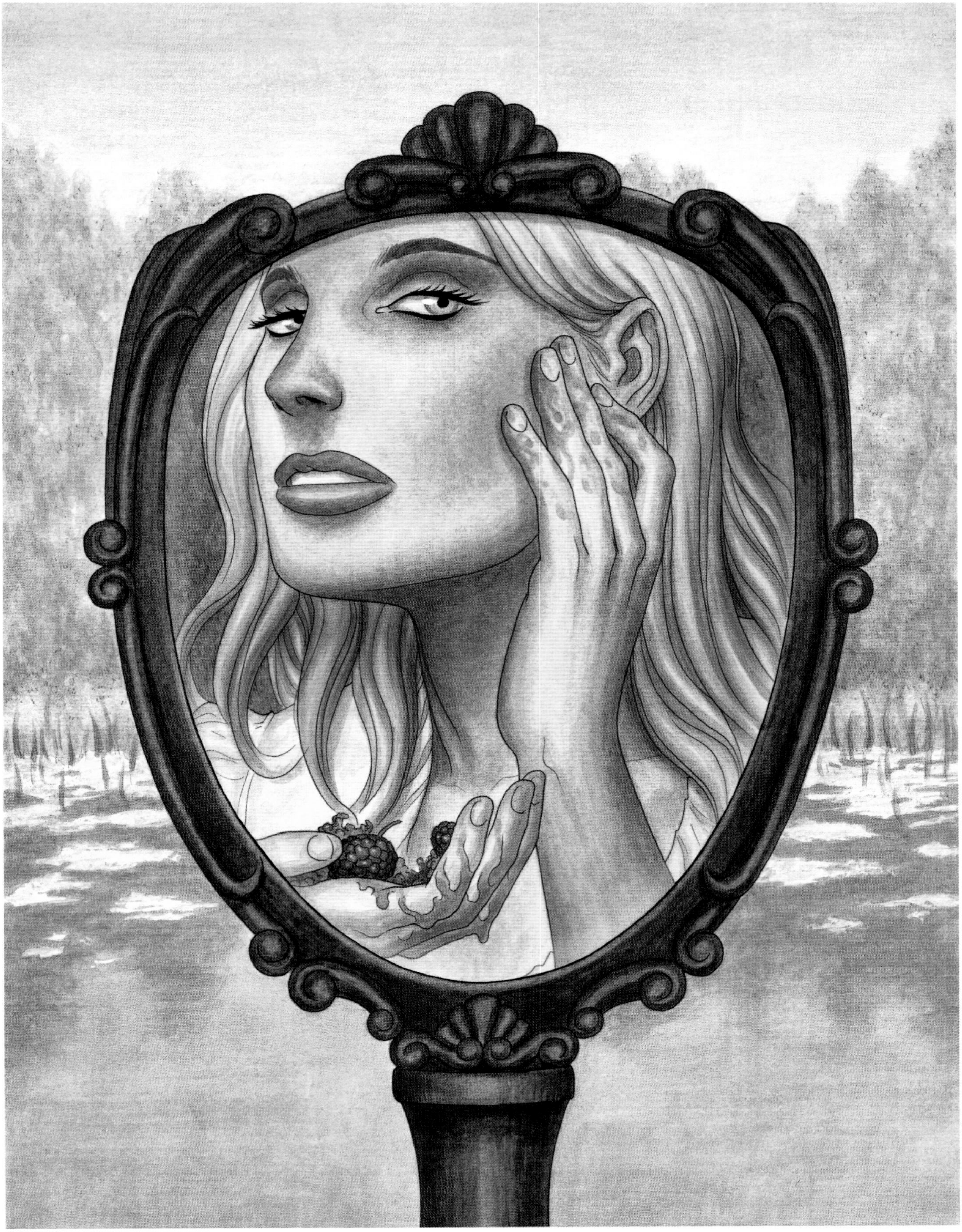

After days of work, Star Bright looked in the pan-stick again and was overjoyed with her newfound beauty.

"I...I look...amazing!" she exclaimed. "I can't believe this beauty was hidden for so long!"

Star Bright spent days gazing at herself in the pan-stick. She didn't speak to her friends, though they were close by her side as usual. This behavior worried and confused the animals.

One day, Toad hopped forward and asked, "Why do you look at yourself all day?"

"Because I'm beautiful," said Star Bright, not moving her eyes away from her reflection. "In fact, there's nothing more beautiful to look at."

"Why don't we do something fun?" asked Owl.

"Let's play a game in the wood!" suggested Capybara.

Star Bright became annoyed and, eyes still on the looking glass, snarled, "I don't want to play with you. Actually, I don't even want to be around any of you. Toad, you're fat and slimy. Owl, you're a big-headed, big-eyed bird. And Capybara, you look like an overgrown bunny rabbit without the adorable ears. You're all ugly creatures, and I want you out of my sight. I would rather be around butterflies, swans, and ponies. I only want to be around beautiful things!"

The animals looked at each other, very puzzled. They had never seen Star Bright act this way before. Hurt from the insults, and having lost such a dear friend, they slouched away to the wood. But before they walked ten little-animal paces, they heard Star Bright scream.

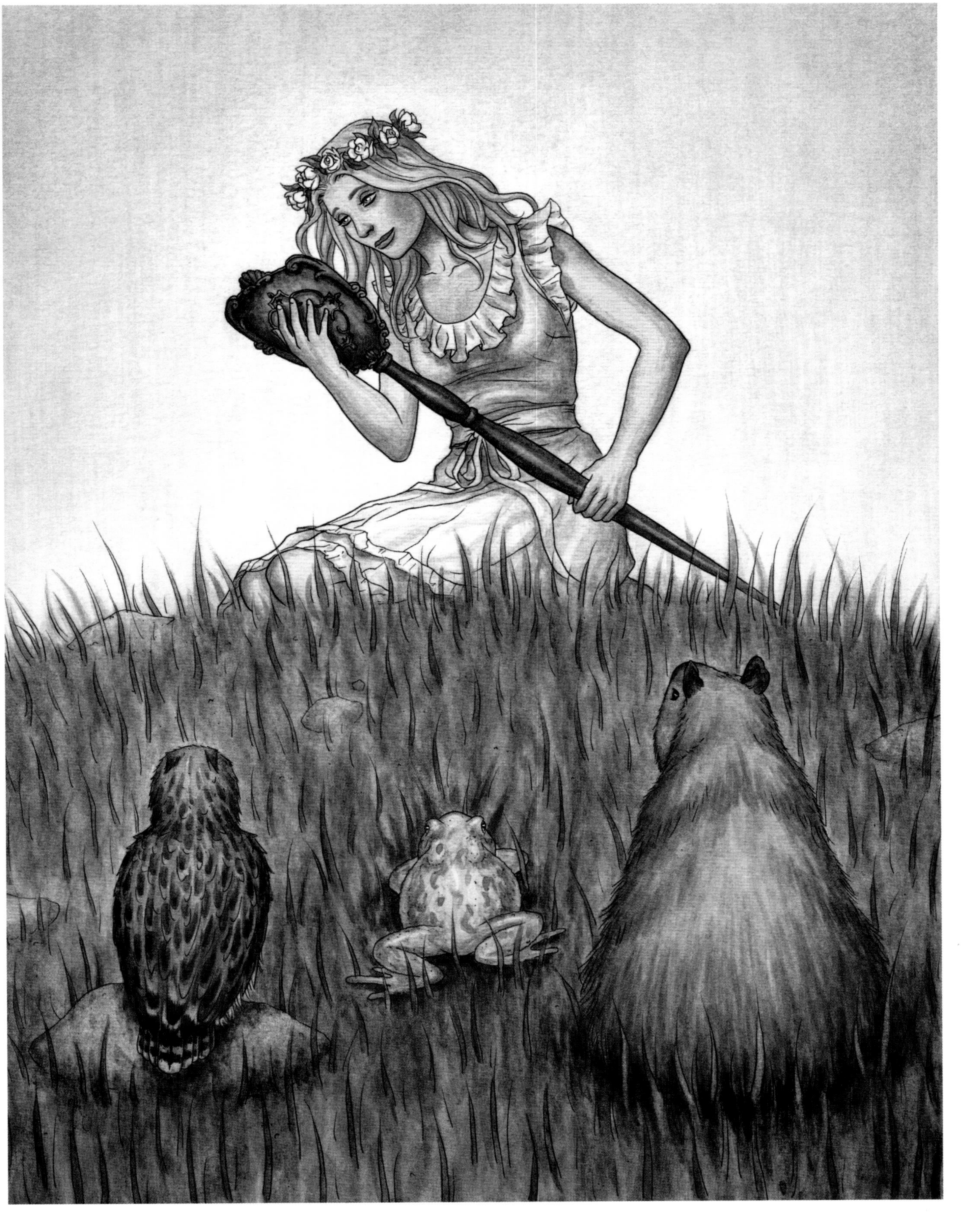

When the animals turned around, they saw black smoke shoot out of the pan-stick. The smoke looked alive, turning into dark, misty ribbons, then into a woman in a long, black robe. She was the ugliest woman Star Bright and the animals had ever seen. Her eyes were almost popping out of her head, her nose was freakishly long and crooked, her mouth was a permanent sneer, and her face had a few unfortunate warts. Star Bright and the animals could barely stand to look at her.

The ugly woman faced Star Bright, smiled, and croaked, "Hello, beautiful girl. I see you've found my looking glass."

"L-looking glass?" stuttered Star Bright. "What's a looking glass? How did you...come out of there?"

"I am Chrona the Sorceress. Have you not heard of me? Well, you *do* live in the wood," said the ugly woman. "What is your name, dear girl?"

"S-Star Bright."

"Star Bright," Chrona slowly repeated. "Very appropriately named." She delicately took the pan-stick from Star Bright's shaking hands and said, "*This* is a looking glass; a mirror. Beautiful girls love looking glasses. However, this particular one is very special. It can do amazing things. For one, I asked it to show me a beautiful maiden, and it showed you. I couldn't tell if you were truly beautiful, so I placed the looking glass here, near the pond, to make sure. And you cleaned up nicely. Quite nicely."

Star Bright squinted and asked, "You've been...spying on me?"

"I have a fountain in my castle that shows me what the looking glass 'sees.' I can travel between them, too," said Chrona. "The reason I'm here...is because I thought you'd be the *perfect* person to help me with something."

"You want me to help you?" Star Bright asked softly.

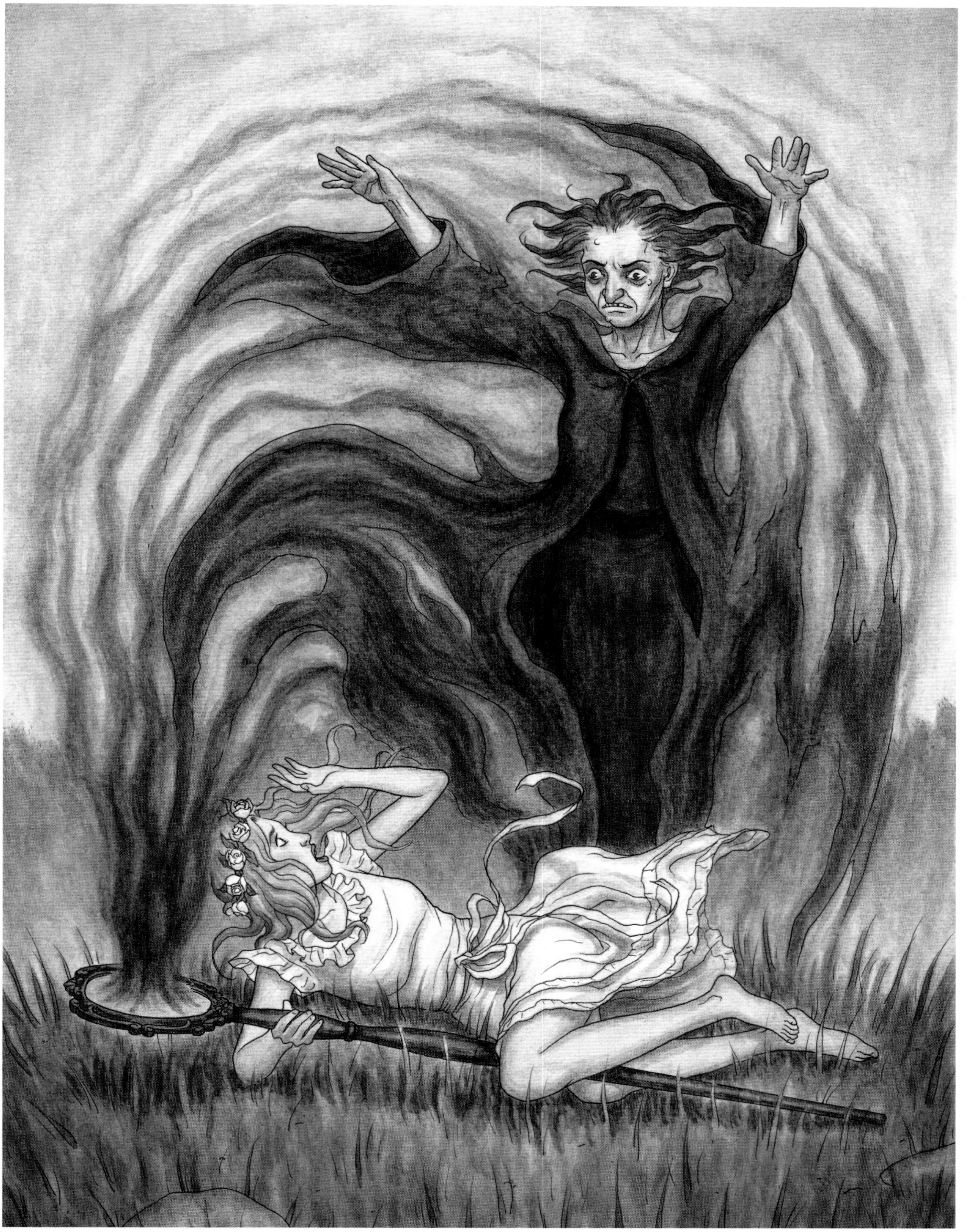

Chrona quickly raised the looking glass, held it between herself and Star Bright, and chanted, "Looking glass, looking glass, spin around; give me the beauty that I have found!"

The looking glass spun and spun, faster and faster, and glowed brighter than any light Star Bright had ever seen. Waves of energy shot out of the looking glass onto Star Bright and Chrona. For a moment, the two were paralyzed, linked by its power.

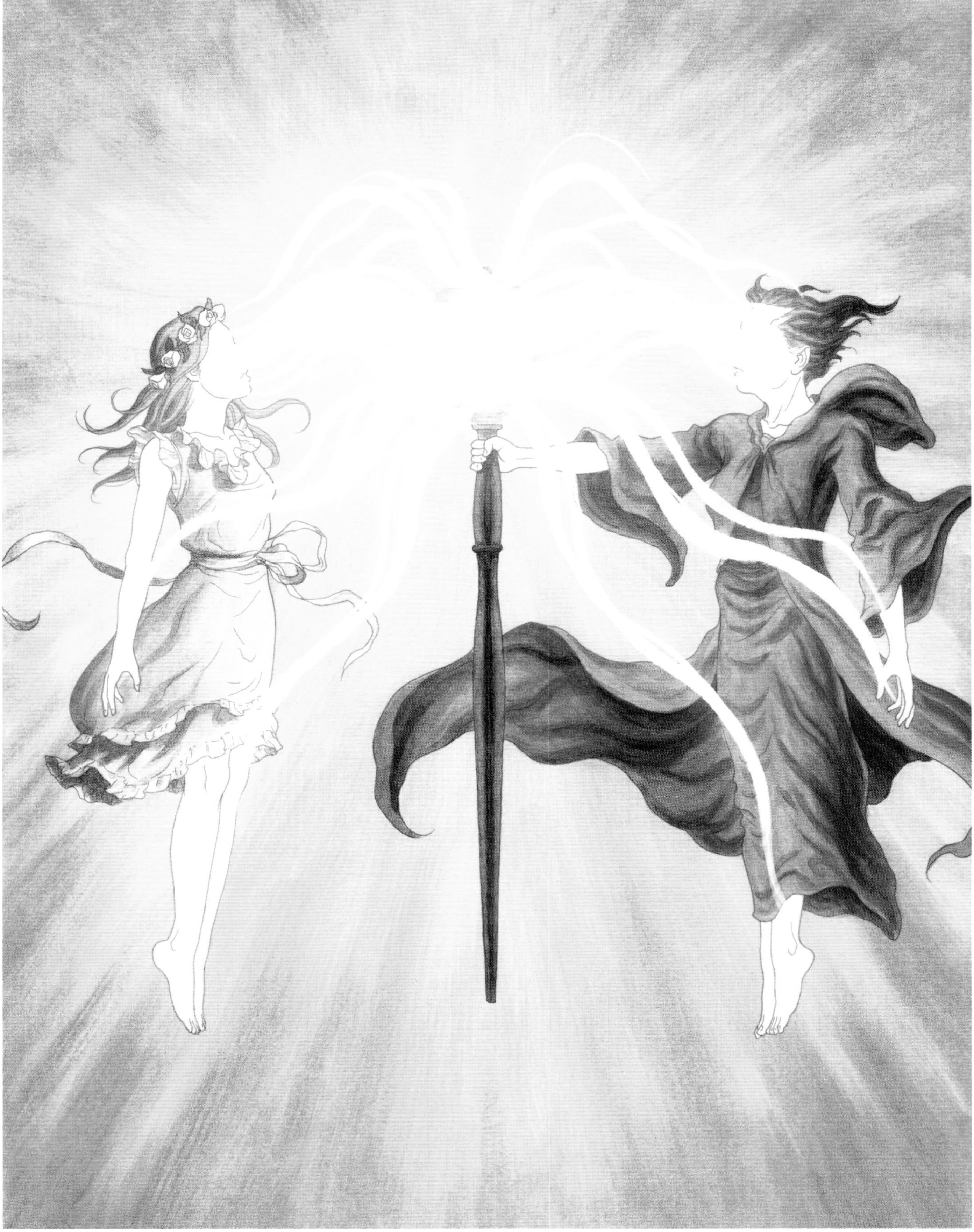

When the light died down, the animals couldn't believe their eyes. Chrona was no longer ugly; she now looked like Star Bright. And Star Bright looked like Chrona. Their bodies had been switched.

Chrona stared into the looking glass and burst into laughter, "I'm beautiful! I'm beautiful! After all of these years, I am so beautiful!"

Star Bright, with trembling hands, felt her face. She looked down at her body and saw Chrona's gray, scraggy form. Eyes wide in shock, she turned to the sorceress and asked, "Why are you doing this?"

Chrona's big smile faded when she pulled her eyes away from the looking glass and turned to Star Bright, the new bearer of her ugly face. After looking at it for decades, she hated to do so for one more second. Chrona began, "Like me, my mother was a sorceress; and, like me, my mother was one of the ugliest people to ever exist. I will never be as great a sorceress as my mother was—it was she who created this looking glass. And after she did, she asked it to show her a beautiful maiden no person cares about, just as I did. My mother became very beautiful—almost as beautiful as I am now. But then she died an untimely death." Chrona paused and stared into the mirror. She began to admire her face again, but then interrupted herself, pushing the mirror aside. "Why am I doing this? Because I deserve better than everyone else." Chrona lifted the looking glass. "And now that I have better, I can't have you trying to take it back."

Chrona swung the looking glass toward the ground. Star Bright quickly lunged forward and grabbed Chrona's arms, but didn't stop them in time. Toad, Owl, and Capybara also moved forward to help, but it was too late. Chrona had struck the looking glass against a rock protruding from the ground.

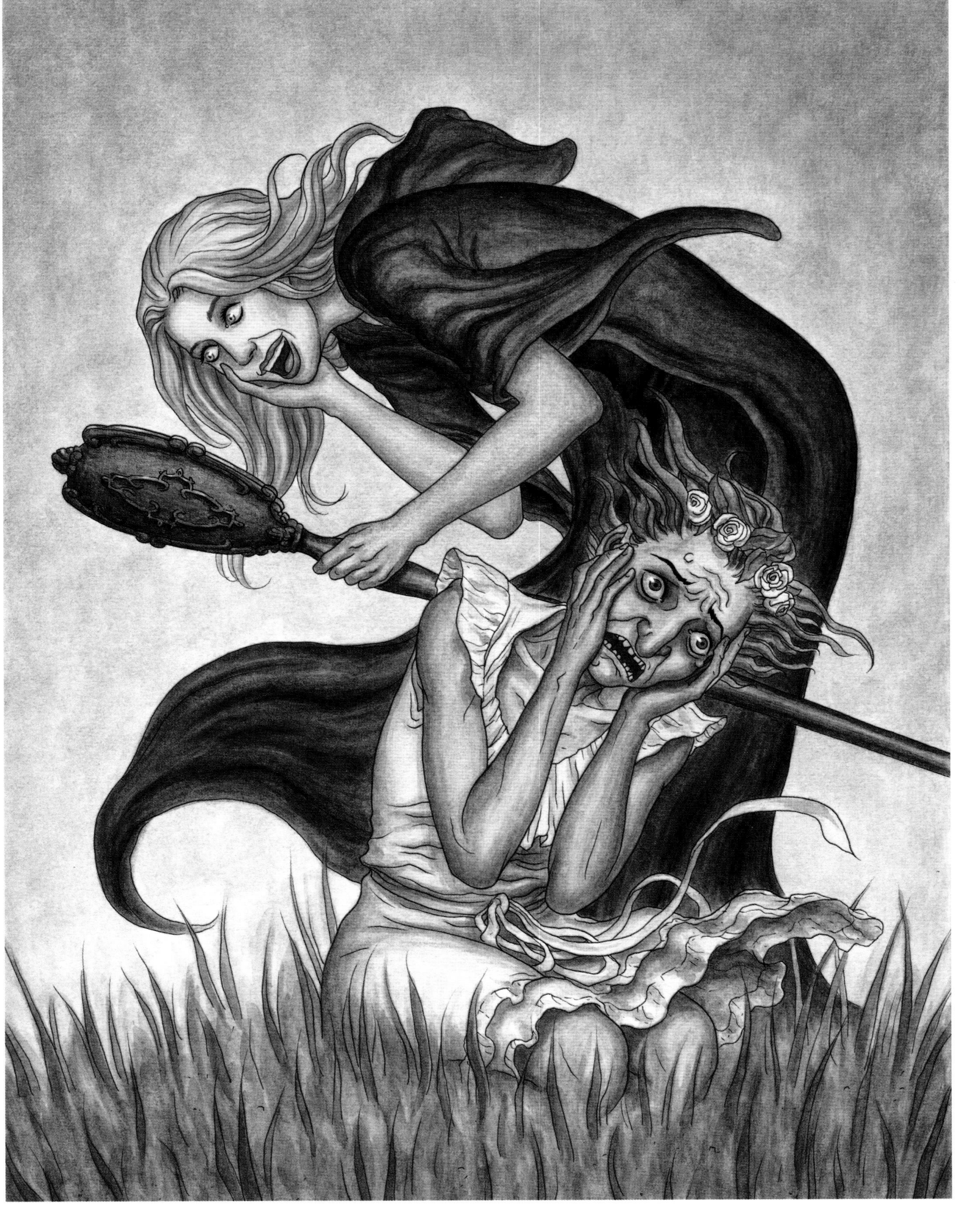

In a blinding flash of light, the glass shattered into pieces. The force of the hit, mixed with the looking glass's magical power, was so strong it sent the shards shooting toward the sky then falling to different parts of the world. The frame and handle were still intact, but only one small piece of glass remained.

Star Bright fell to her knees in despair, and Chrona fled.

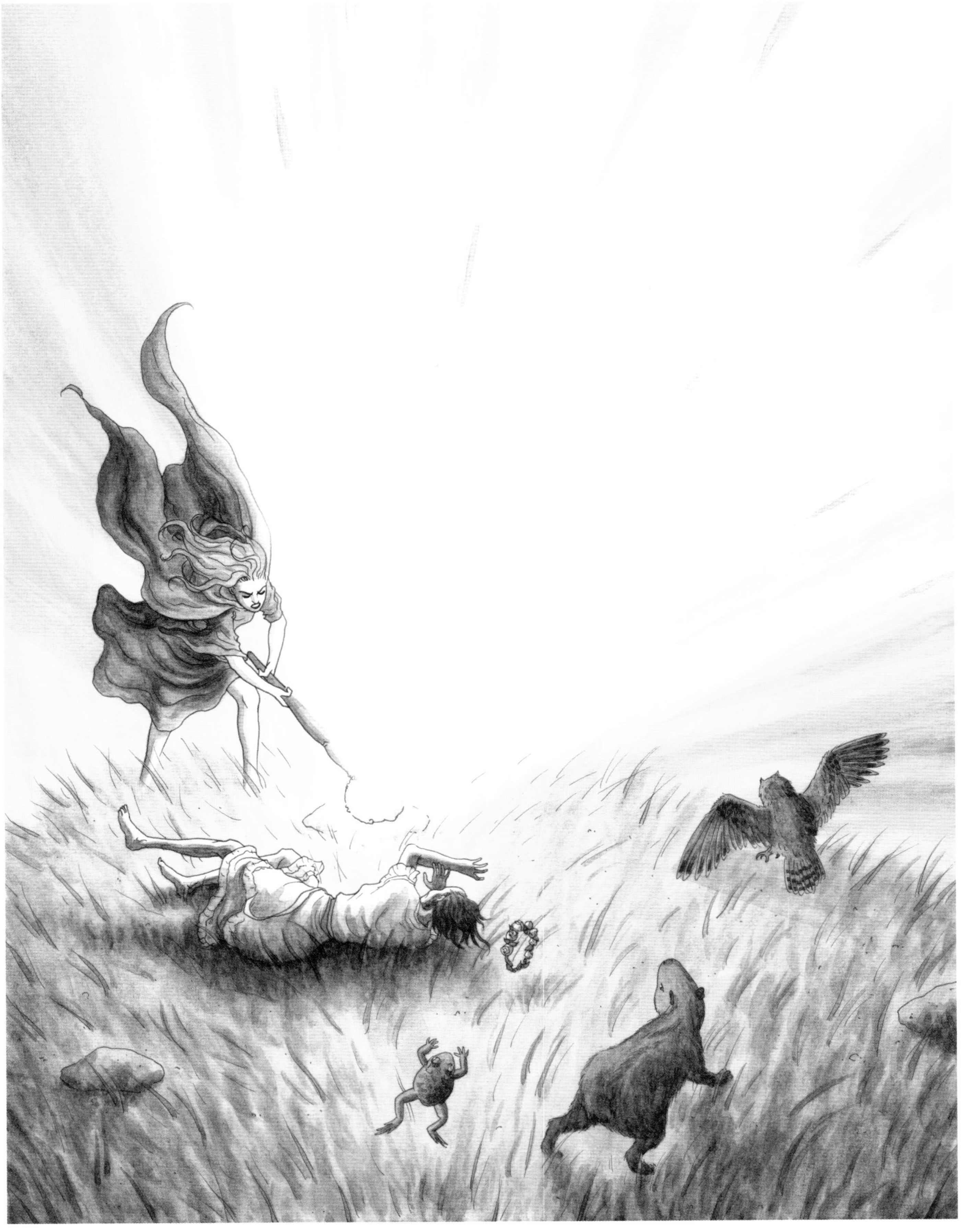

Star Bright went into hiding.

Tales began to spread among travelers that a very ugly woman lived in a cave at the edge of the wood, weeping and sobbing all day, and sometimes all night. The cave caused Star Bright's mournful wailing to echo out into the wood, frightening animals away. She left the cave only to find food and water. Sometimes, travelers came upon her and ran away in terror, or said hurtful things like, "What sort of creature are you?!" or, "Scram, beast, scram!" This caused her to run back to her cave and cry even more and even louder.

Toad, Owl, and Capybara saw what Star Bright was going through. They were hurt by her insults and commands to stay away from her, but they knew she needed a friend—or three.

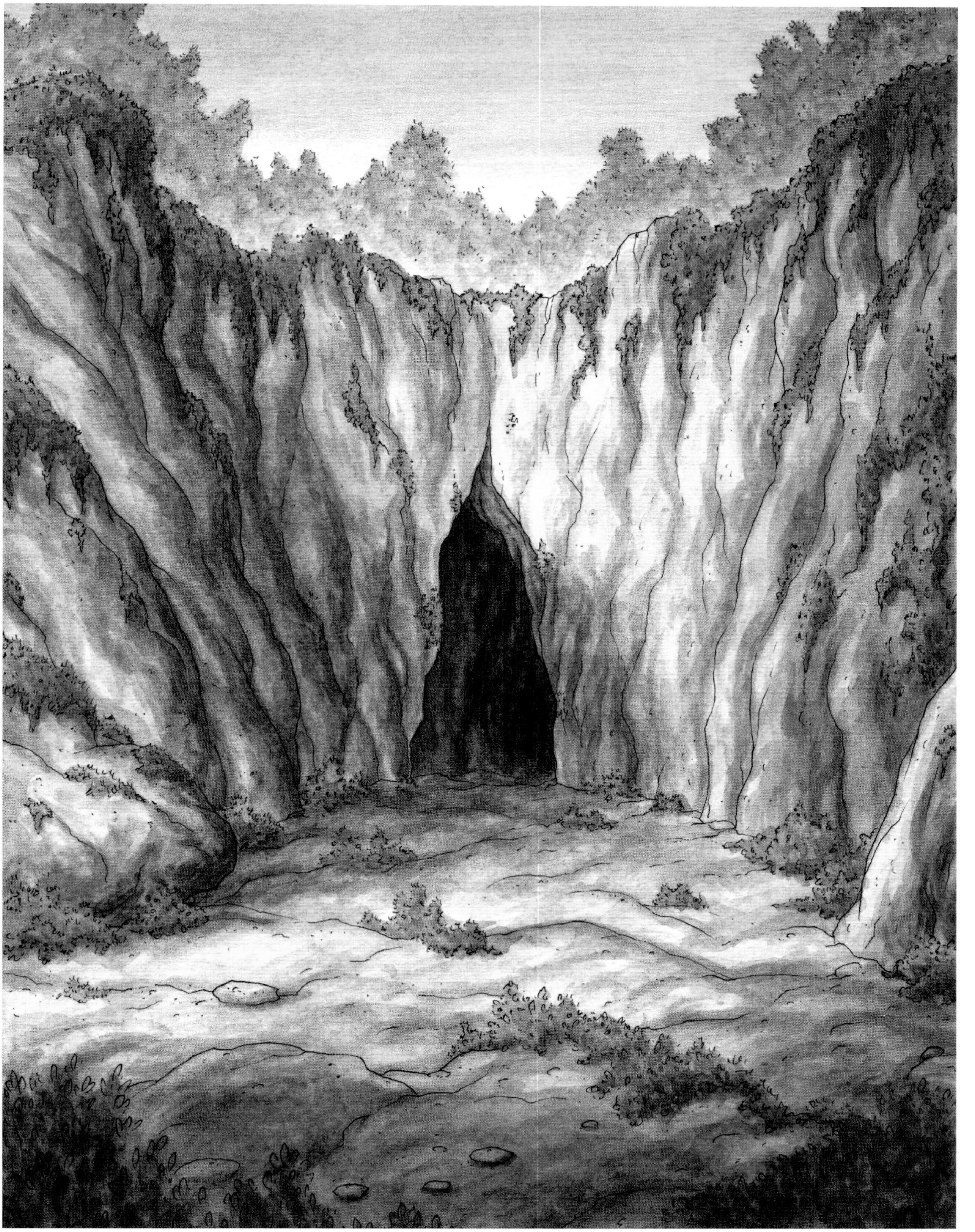

Toad, Owl, and Capybara followed the echoing whimpers to the end of the cave where they found Star Bright huddled up and crying against the farthest wall, hugging the broken looking glass. It still shocked the animals to see her with a different body.

"Star Bright?" whispered Owl.

Star Bright saw that Toad, Owl, and Capybara stood before her, and she quickly covered her face in shame. Eventually, she lowered her hands to look at her friends, tears pouring from her eyes. The animals looked back at her in sadness.

"I used to be so beautiful," Star Bright sniveled. "I am so ugly."

The animals just stood there and listened to her. It was also bizarre for them to hear her speak in a deep, raspy voice—not the soft one that she used to have.

She lightly shook the looking glass and said, "It's broken. I'm going to look like this for the rest of my life."

The animals glanced at each other. After a pause, Owl said, "We've brought something for you."

With her face wet from tears, Star Bright looked confused. Then she noticed that something in Toad's mouth was glowing.

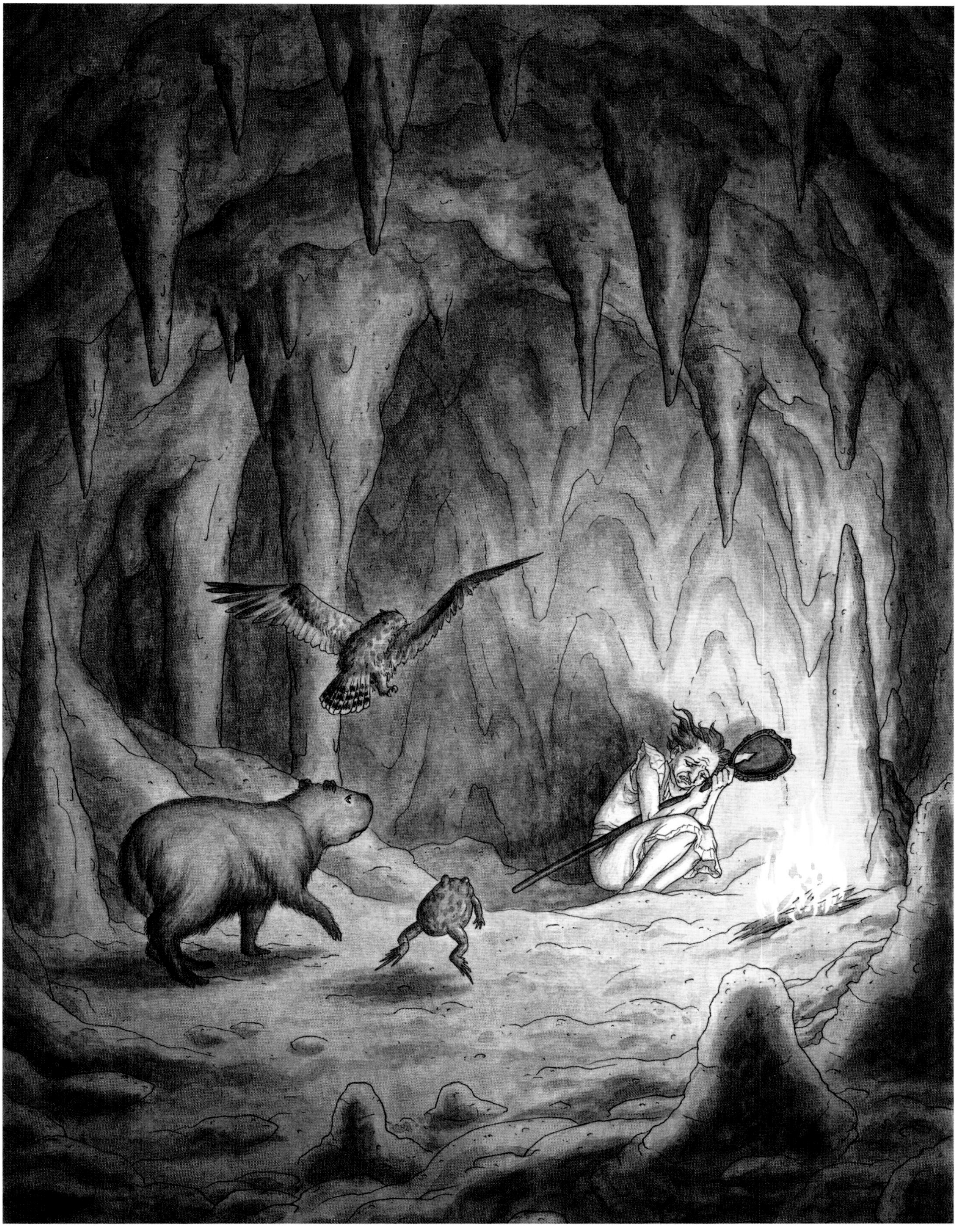

Toad opened his mouth and rolled out his tongue. Within it was a small shard that had been flung from the looking glass.

"It was lying not far from the pond!" Capybara chimed in.

To everyone's surprise, both shards were emitting a glow.

The tongue-tied toad said, "Looh ah thah! Theh thining!"

"They must be shining because they're close to each other!" Capybara observed.

Star Bright delicately took the shard from Toad and found that it fit next to the remaining piece on the looking glass. Before their eyes, the two pieces melded together in an even brighter glow, which then subsided altogether. The four were amazed.

Star Bright slowly stood up with the looking glass in her hands and said, "It was broken, but perhaps it can still be of some use. I can find the missing shards with the help of the looking glass itself. And when I find them, maybe I will be able to fix it and somehow get my beauty back. I must be beautiful again!"

Before Star Bright could take a step forward, Owl said, "You will need more help."

"We feel horrible that you, our dearest friend, had your beauty stolen," said Capybara. "We want to help you find the shards, no matter where they are in the world."

Star Bright was struck by how unconditionally loyal her friends were, even after she treated them so badly. Her face became red with shame and her eyes darted about the ground. She felt she should say something to give thanks. But pride got in the way. All she could muster was a quiet, "Alright."

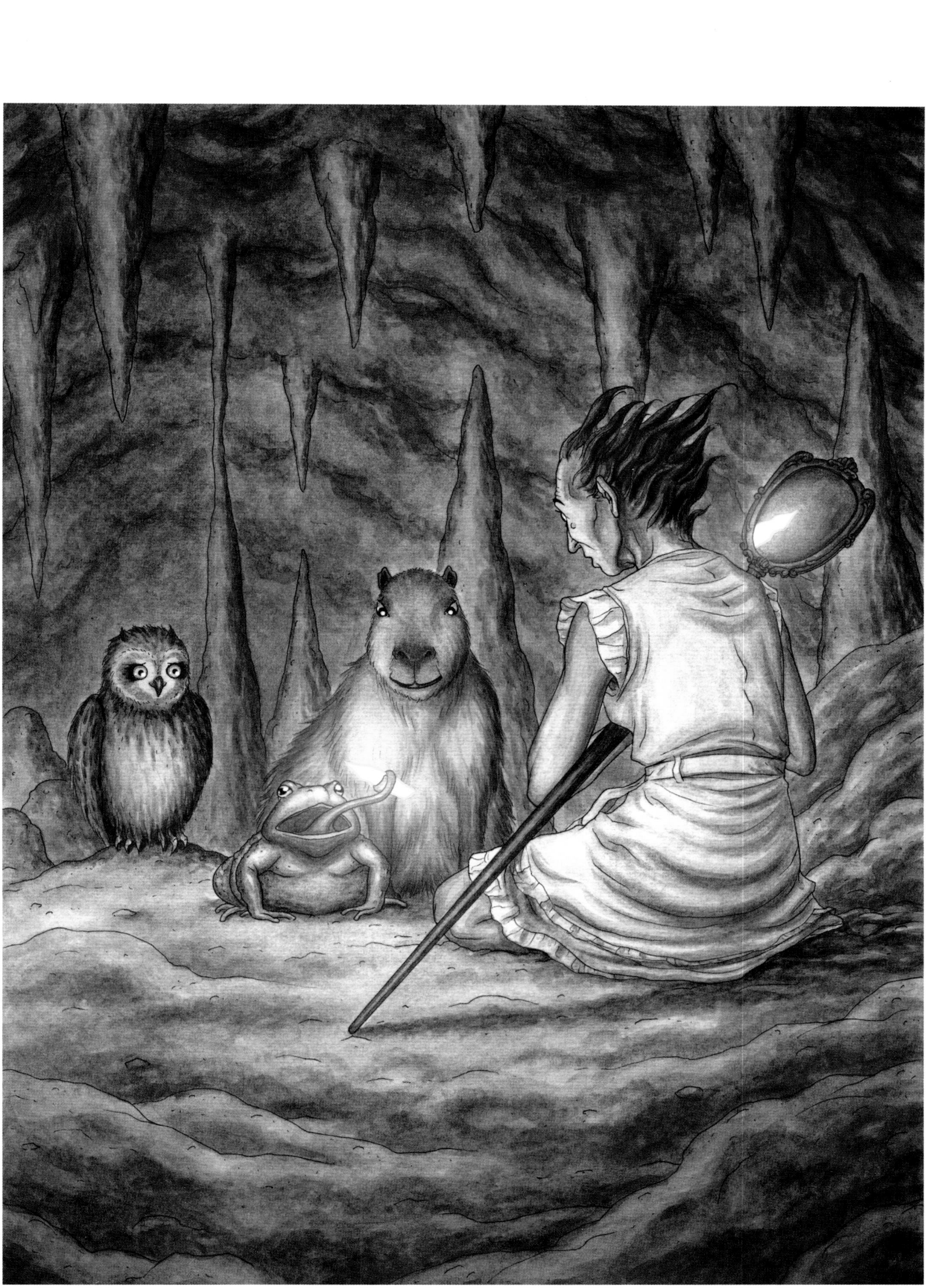

Star Bright and the animals left the wood and headed out in search of the missing shards.

Star Bright used the broken looking glass as a walking stick and hiked ahead of Toad, Owl, and Capybara. A fly buzzed around her face, and she tried to swat it with her hand, saying, "Ew! Flies are gross!" While she was distracted, the animals took the moment to talk amongst themselves.

Toad said, "Star Bright was mean to us. And I don't like the way she is with the looking glass. Why are we helping her?"

"She *was* mean to us," Owl responded, "but she's our friend. If this is what she wants, we should help her." Capybara nodded in agreement.

Toad wasn't sure if he agreed, but he hopped along with Owl and Capybara anyway.

As they journeyed, Owl flew high above, looking for anything that glowed. A shard would shine brightly if the looking glass was near it.

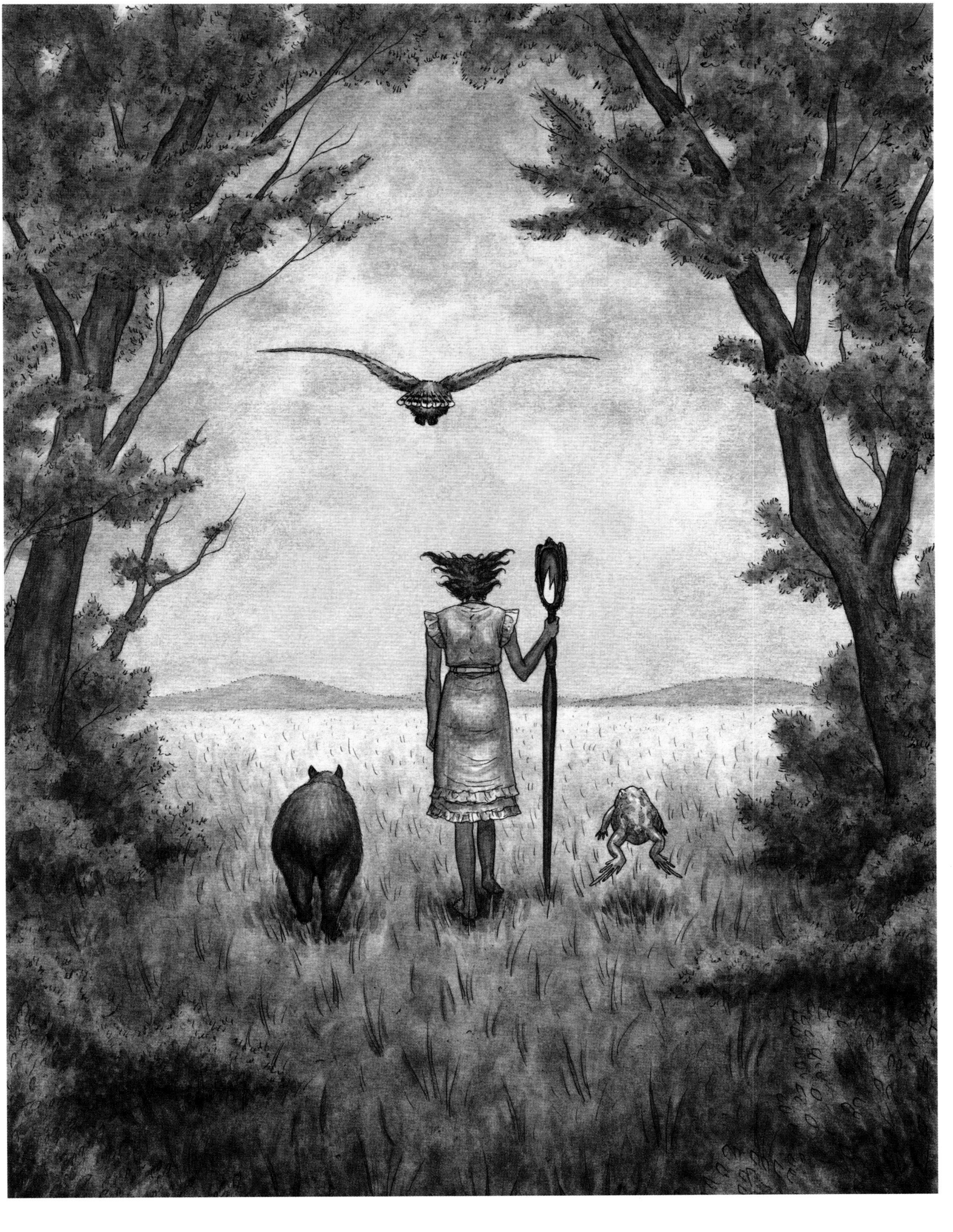

In the hills of the grasslands, Owl spotted a glowing shard from miles away.

When they reached the shard, Star Bright added it to the looking glass. Again, the pieces merged in a bright glow.

"Oh, Star Bright," Owl said as he landed on her shoulder, "if only I could search the world by myself and save all of you the trouble, I would, but the looking-glass shards are too big and slippery for my small beak and claws."

"It's no matter," she said. "You can spot the littlest things from so far away. We wouldn't be able to find the shards at all, if not for your big, beautiful eyes."

The fluffy owl hooted with joy, and flew a little higher that day.

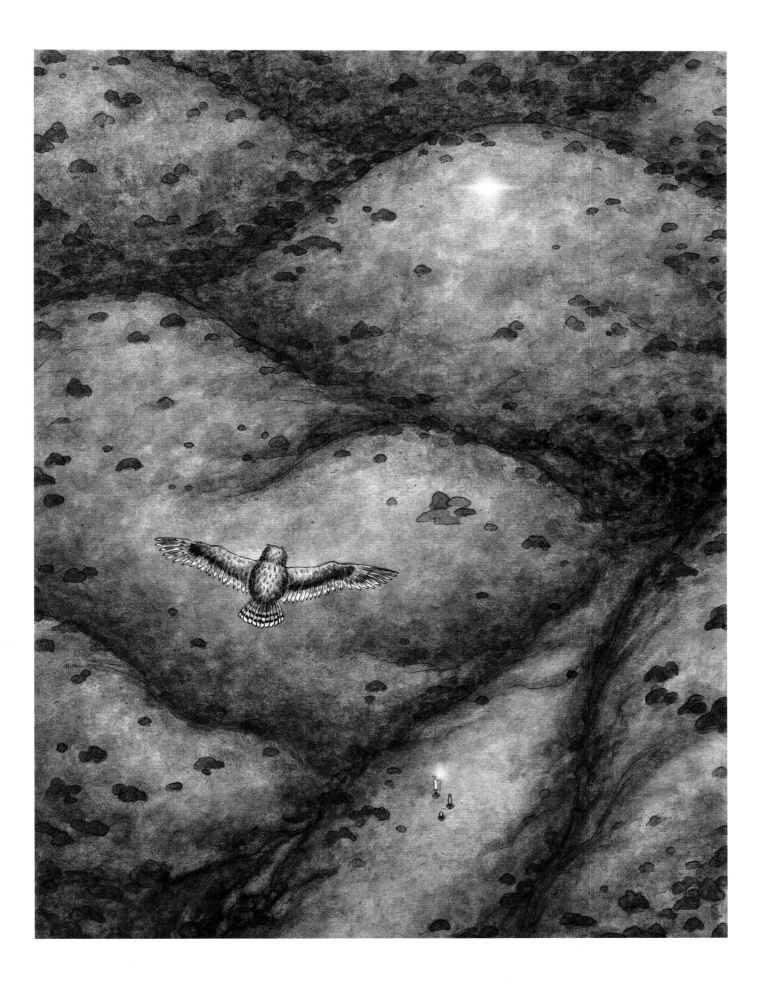

They found another shard glowing in the sea, not far from the coast.

Toad said, "I love the water, but Capybara is actually a much better swimmer than I."

Capybara jumped into the ocean and dove deep toward the light.

When Capybara returned to the shore with the shard, Star Bright said to him, "You're an amazing swimmer. You have the perfect body for diving."

The furry capybara snorted with joy, and trotted a little faster that day.

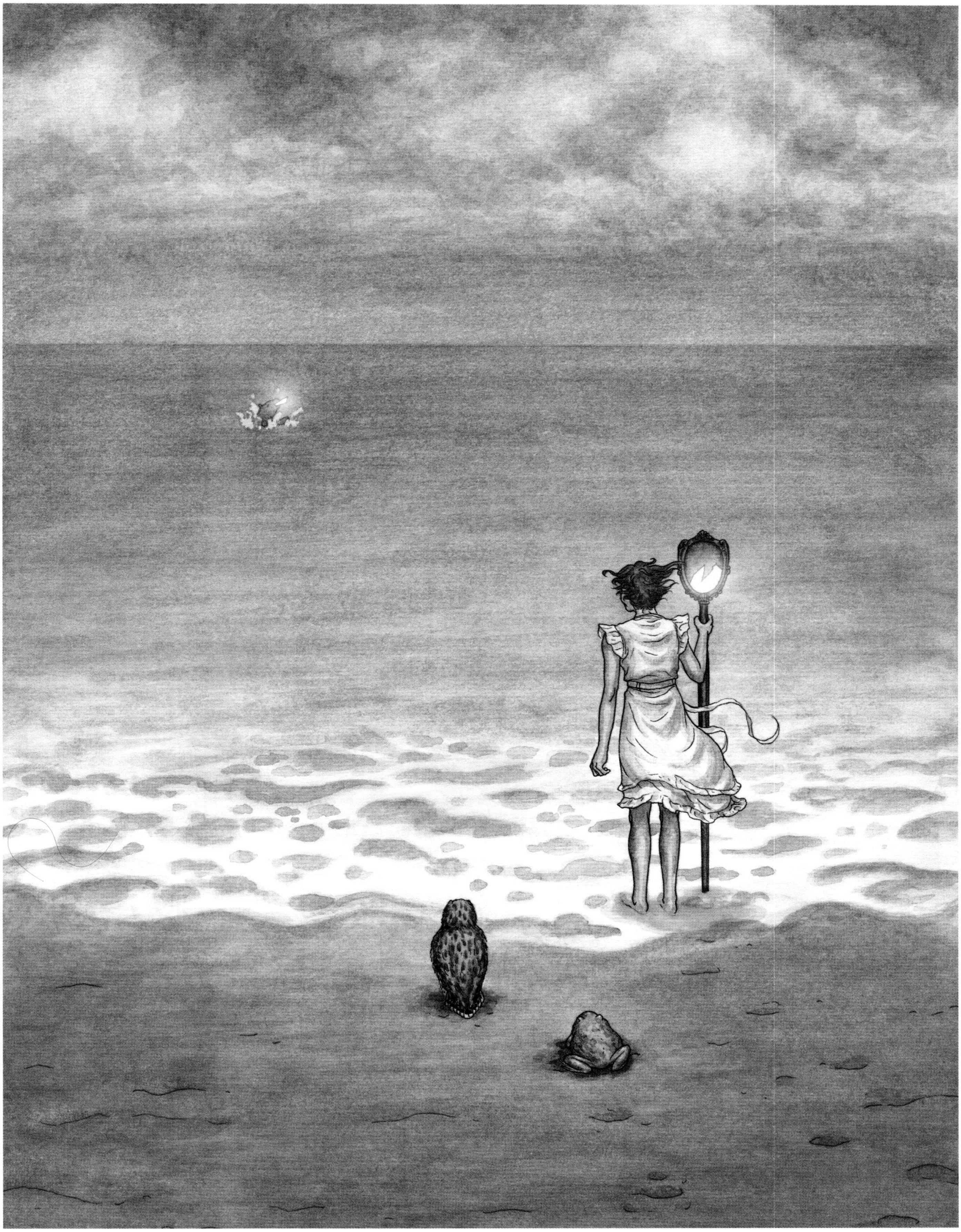

In the heart of a deep crevice among large rock formations rested another shard.

Only Toad was small and slippery enough to get to it.

"Be careful!" shouted Star Bright, from the top of the crevice.

When Toad returned with the shard, wrapped within his tongue, Star Bright said to him, "You're so good at squeezing through things. If it wasn't for you being little and slippery, we never would have gotten this piece."

The chubby toad croaked with joy, and hopped a little farther that day.

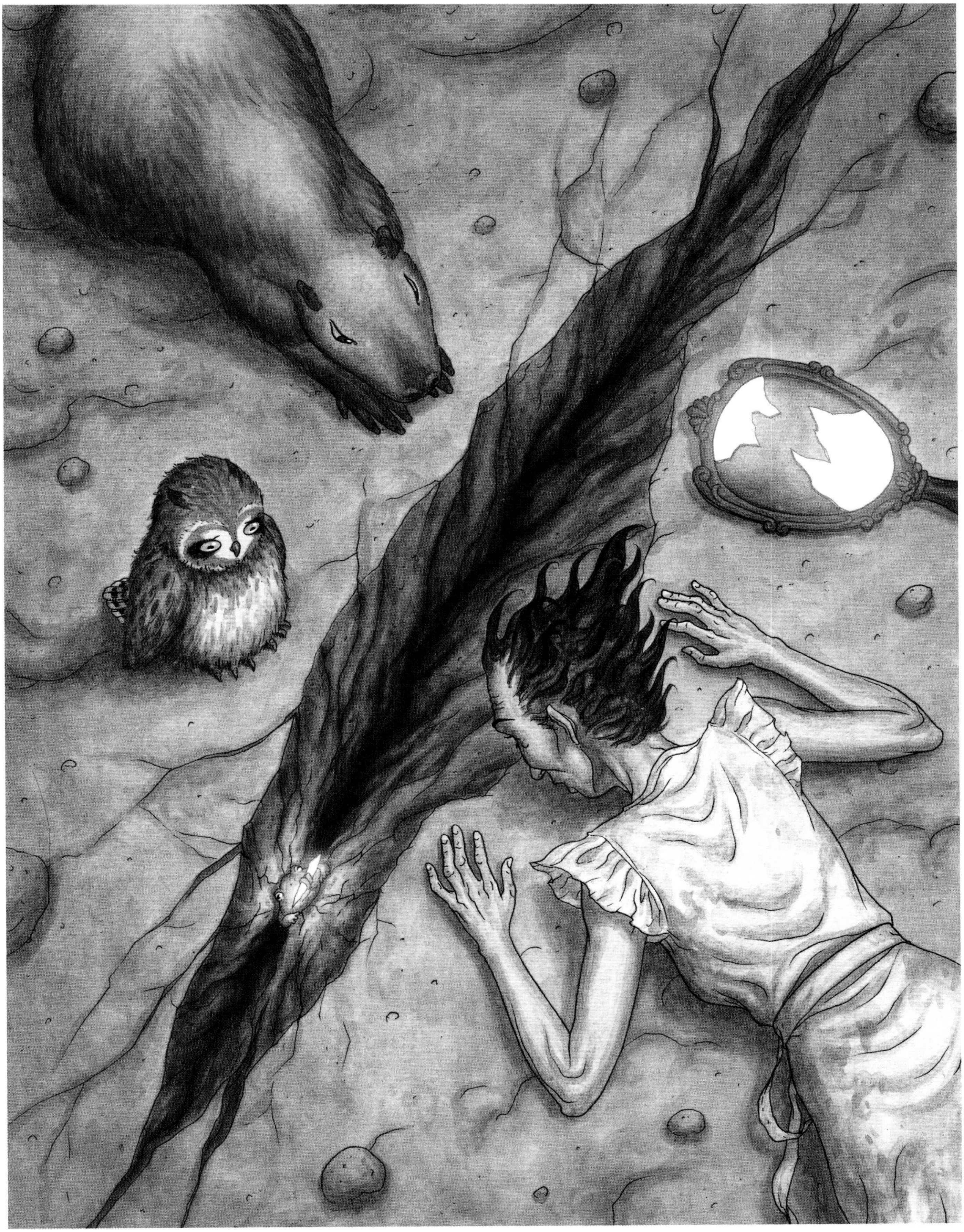

Among the tall, wet trees of a tropical rainforest, they encountered a shard resting on a high branch. Living in the wood her whole life, Star Bright was great at climbing trees, but with Chrona's body, she wasn't as fit as she used to be. Slowly, she clambered up one of the tallest trees to get the shard.

It was raining lightly throughout the forest. When Star Bright returned from the tree, she and the animals tilted their heads back and opened their mouths to replenish themselves. Watching her friends quietly drinking, her eyes began to well up with tears. She fell to her knees and cried, "Oh, dear Toad, dear Owl, dear Capybara, I am so sorry for what I said! I'm sorry for hurting your feelings! What I did was so wrong, and I will never be so awful again! Would you please forgive me?"

The animals looked at each other, then back at Star Bright.

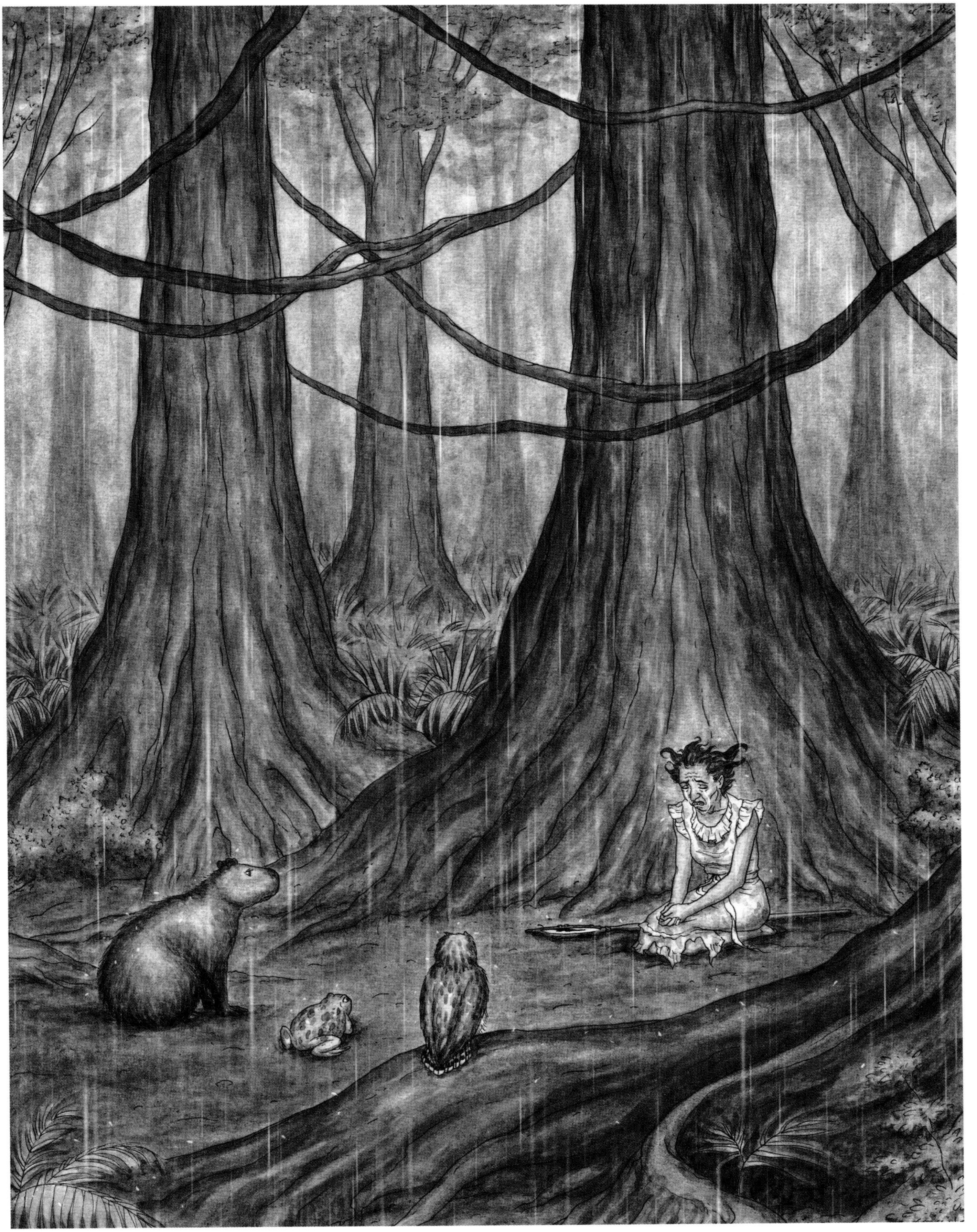

"Of course we forgive you," Owl said. "You're our friend." Capybara and Toad smiled.

Star Bright's face relaxed with relief, and her shoulders slumped as if she had let go of something extremely heavy.

Suddenly, Capybara hopped, shook his fur, and sprayed water all over everyone.

"Eek!" Star Bright laughed. The four friends played in the rain for a while. Star Bright reminisced about playing games with Toad, Owl, and Capybara in the wood, and the animals enjoyed seeing her smile again, even if it wasn't with the same face.

Piece by piece, the looking glass was coming together.

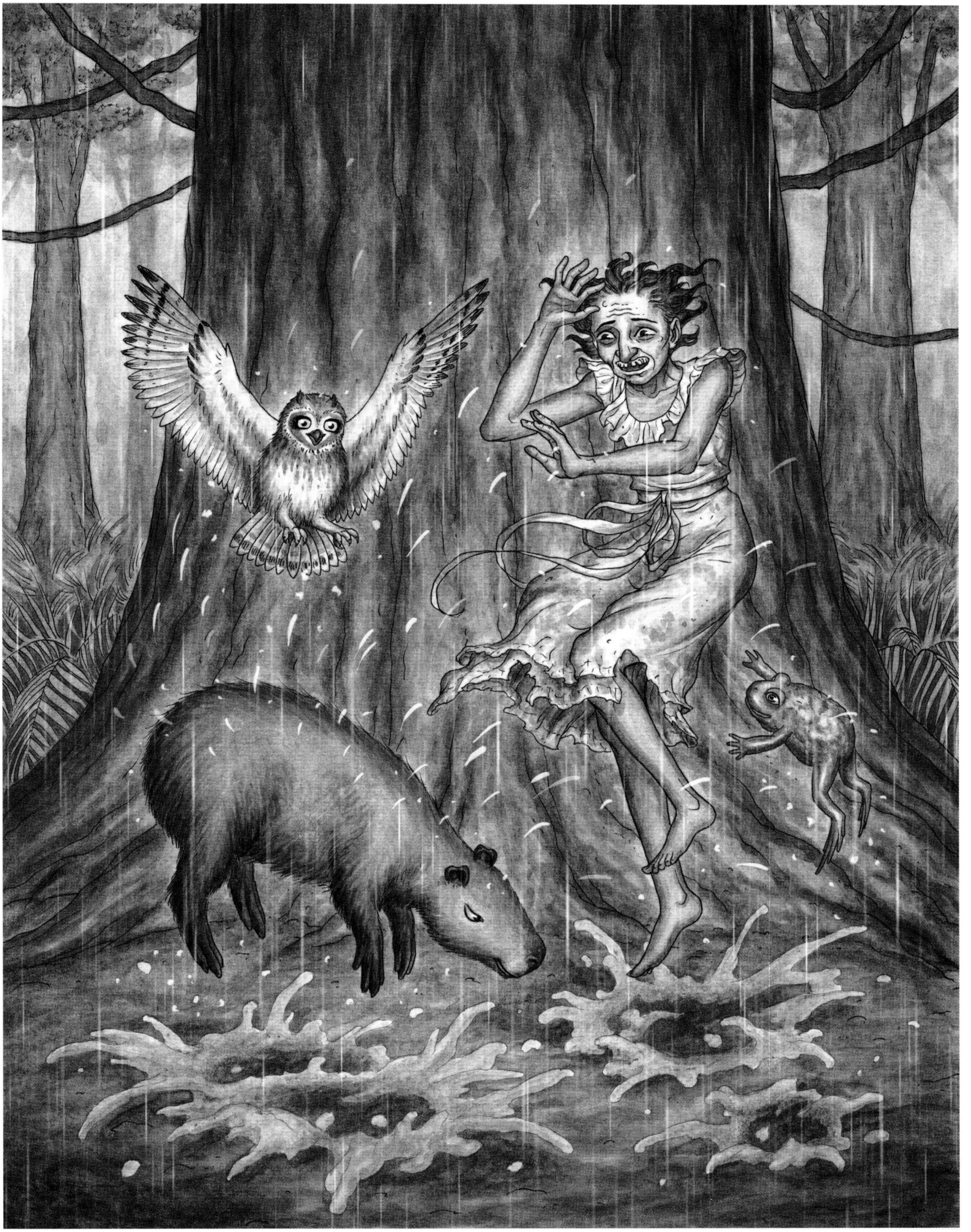

They discovered another shard on a dune in the blistering desert.

It was the hottest, driest place that Star Bright and the animals had ever set foot in. Though they had just come from the rainforest, they quickly became thirsty and had to rest in any shade they could find between dunes. Toad was almost cooked, so Star Bright held him against her chest to shield him from the sweltering sun. The journey was arduous, but Toad was very glad to have come along on it.

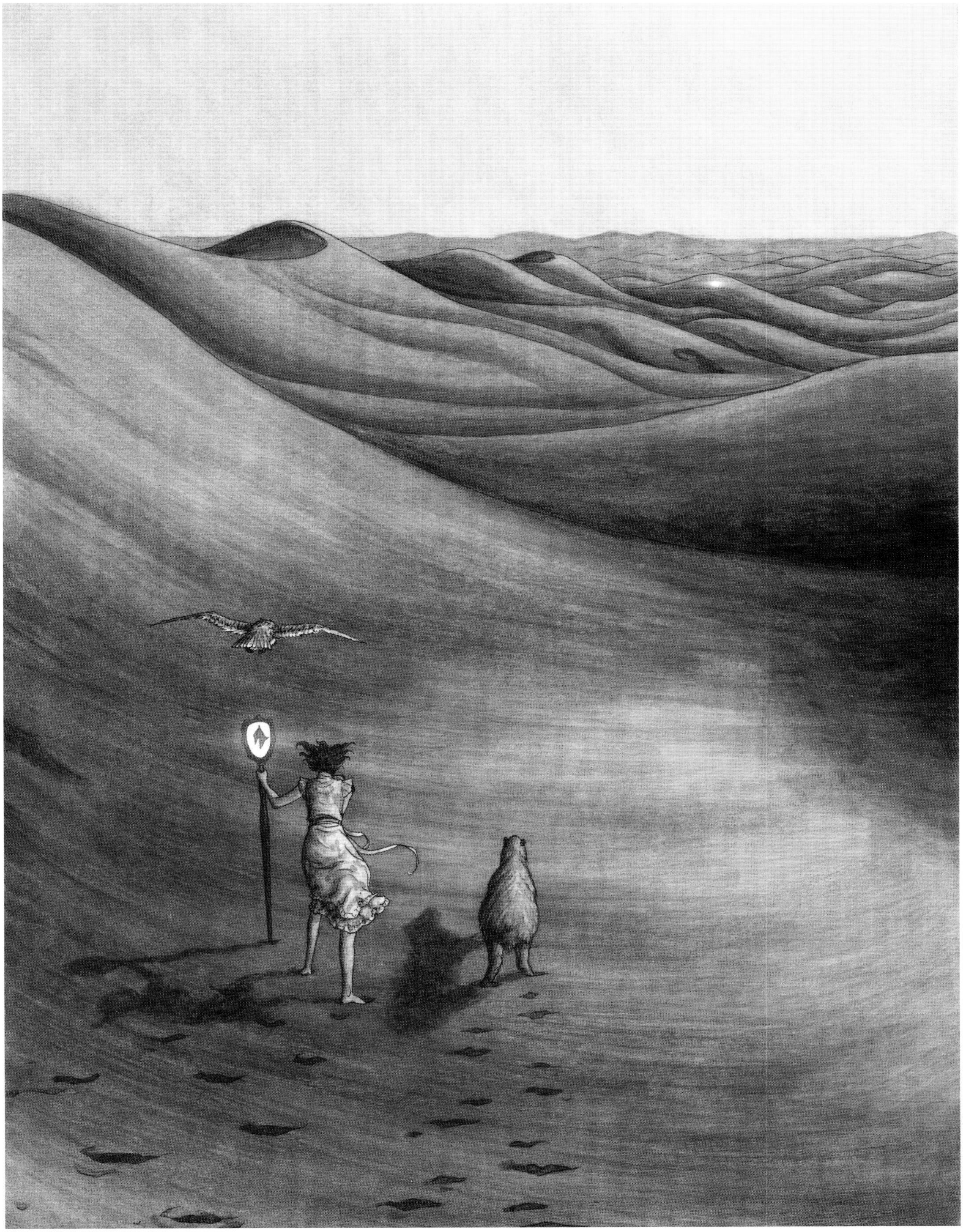

The final shard lay at the top of an icy mountain.

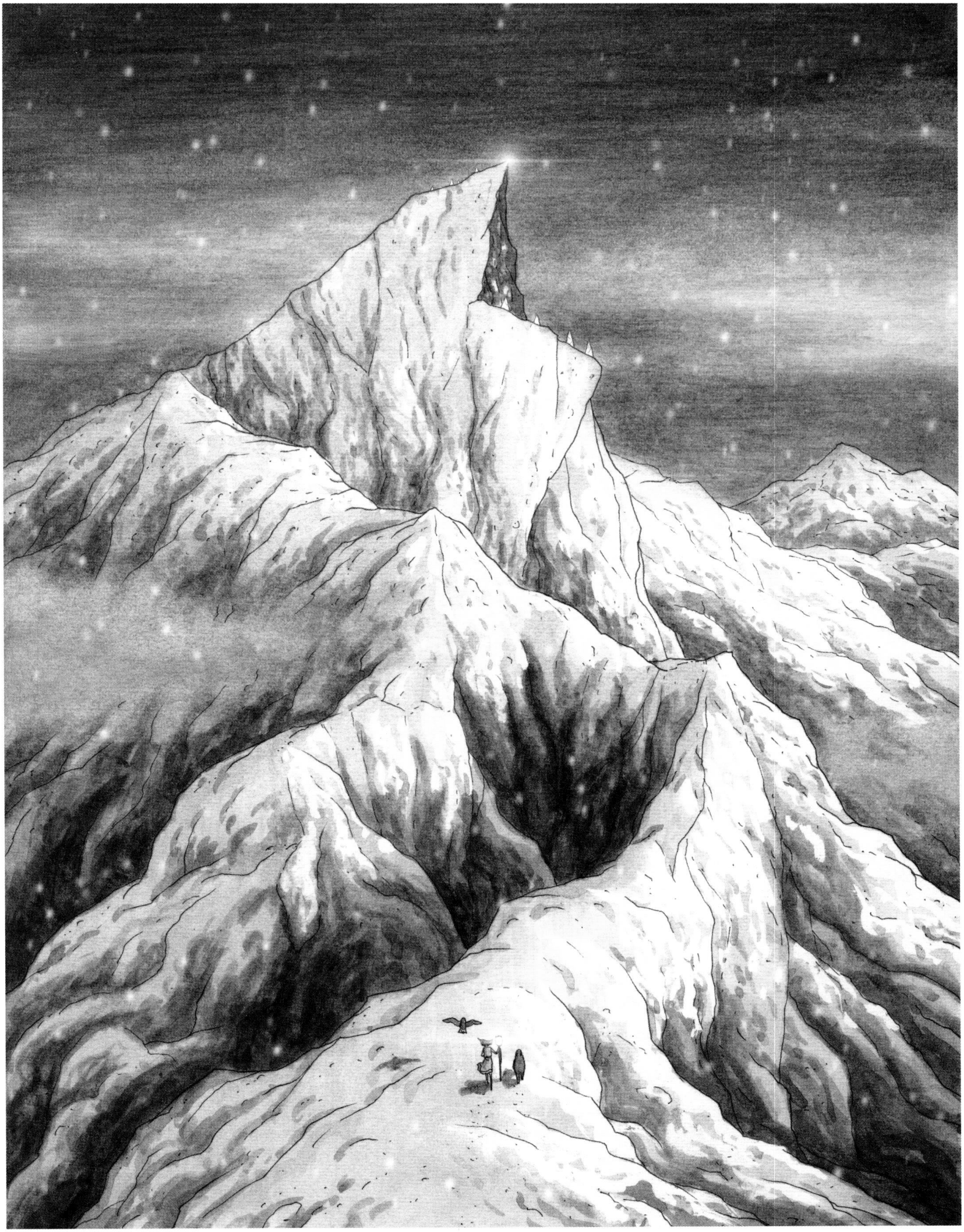

Snow fell and clouds covered the sky, blocking the sun's heat. After walking in a huddle to reach the top of the mountain, they approached the final shard and saw it lying on a frozen spike just below the sheer cliff of the mountain. The shard was small, and a gust of wind could have blown it away. Far below the cliff were even larger ice spikes.

"If all four of us work together—linking up and hanging from the cliff—we could reach it!" said Capybara.

Star Bright looked down from the precipice and surveyed the situation. "No," she said. "It's too dangerous. We could all die." She paused, then turned to her friends. "Thank you so much for journeying with me...but I'd rather live the rest of my life in this body than lose any of you." With a sore heart, she placed the looking glass on the ground and said, "Let's go back home."

The animals didn't want to accept Star Bright's decision, but she insisted. And the longer they stayed on the icy mountaintop, the colder they were getting. So they headed home.

Leading her friends back down the mountain, Star Bright said, "It's so cold. Can we walk in a huddle again?" Star Bright looked behind her, and her friends were not there.

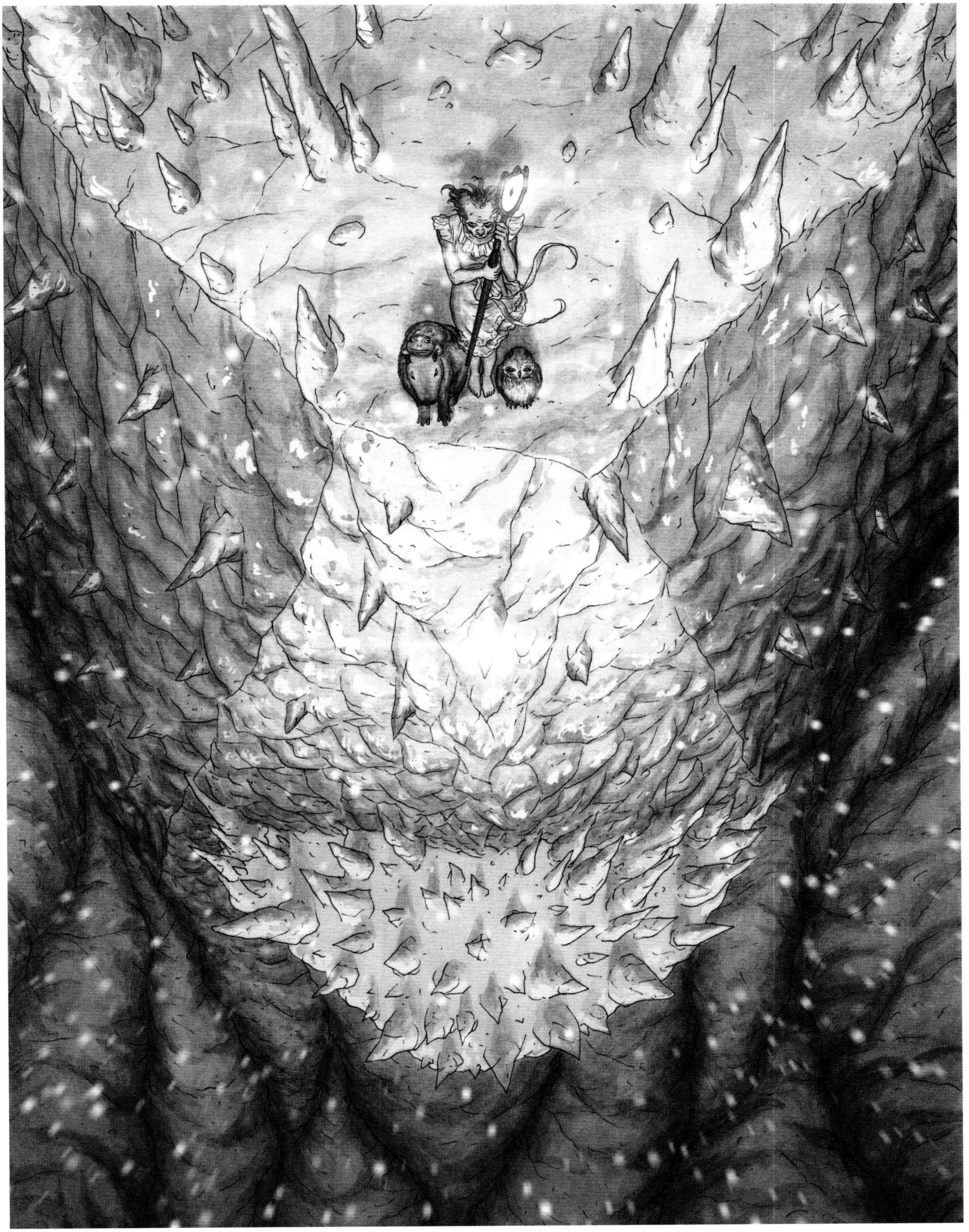

Star Bright ran back up the mountain and saw Capybara hanging from the cliff, Owl hanging from Capybara, and Toad hanging from Owl. Just as she reached them, Capybara's little webbed forefeet slipped from the icy edge, and all the animals began to fall. Star Bright caught one of Capybara's feet just within reach and was almost pulled off the cliff. She heaved as hard as she could. Slowly, she brought the animals back up to safety.

Panting and lying on the ice with the animals, Star Bright noticed that something in Toad's mouth was glowing.

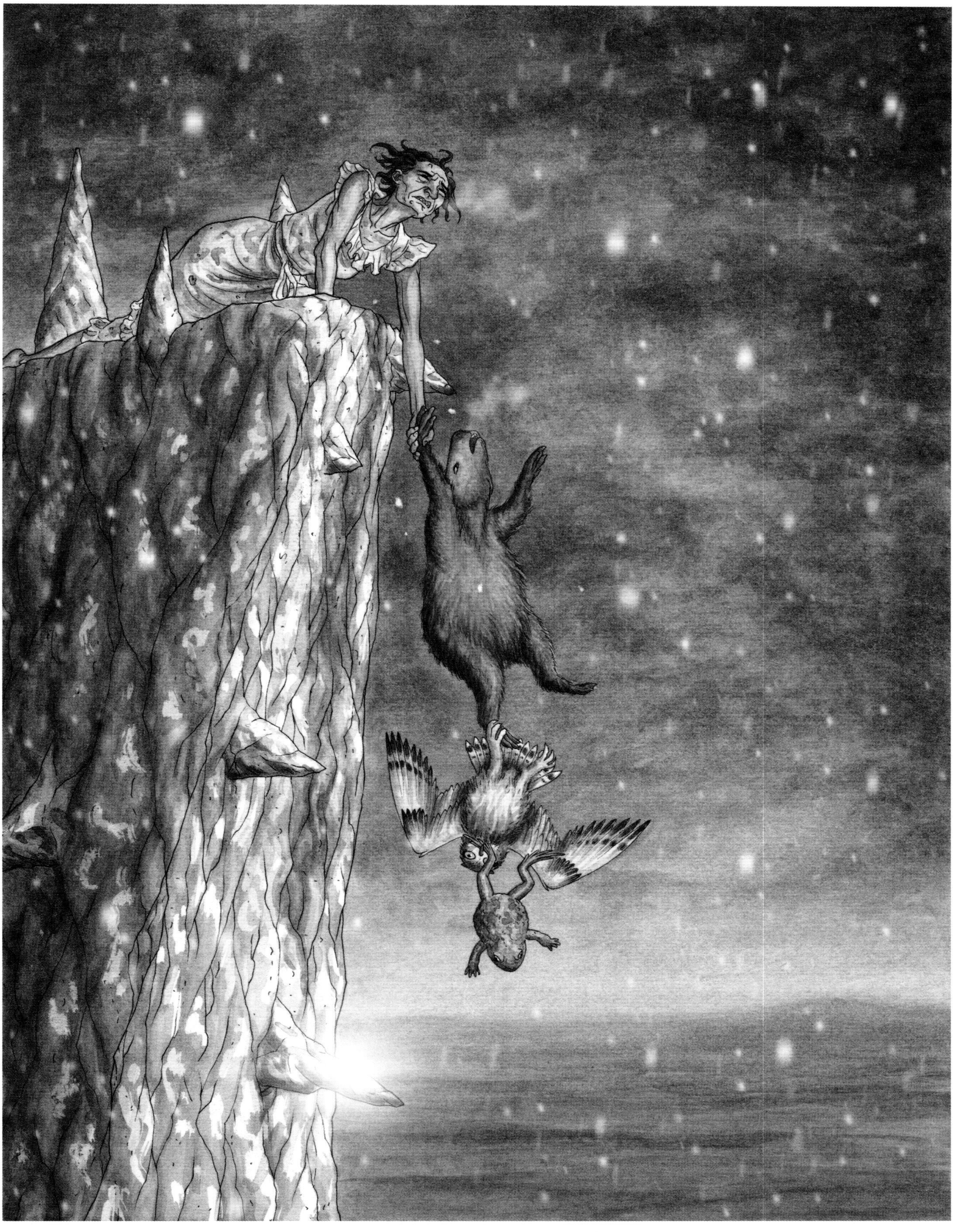

Star Bright held the broken looking glass and last shard in her hands. She and the animals stood together, thinking about how far they had come to find all of the shards. Holding her breath, Star Bright snapped the piece in its place, and the entire looking glass glowed with intense brightness. When the light subsided, the looking glass was complete again, as perfect as it was when Star Bright found it.

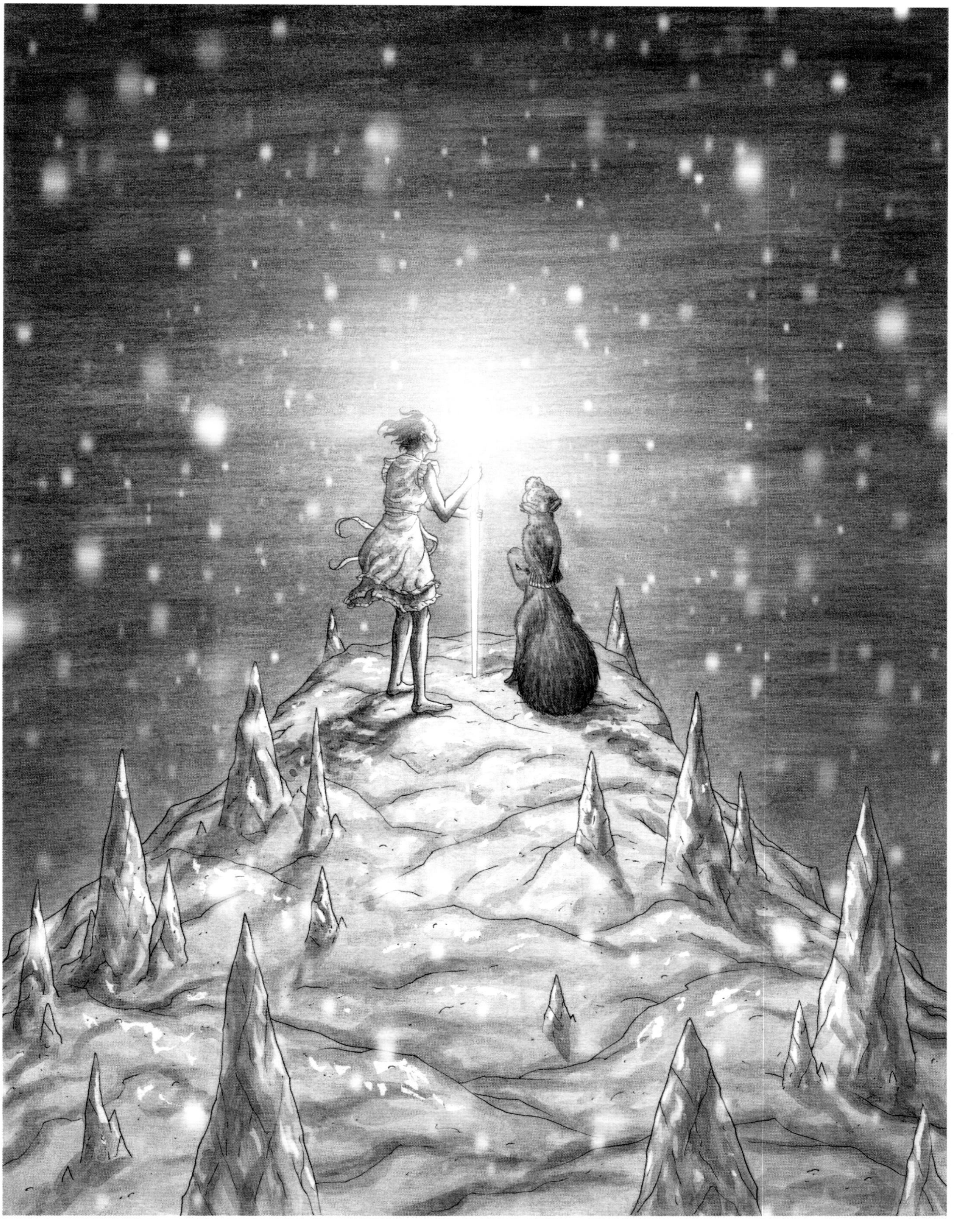

Now that the looking glass was fixed, Star Bright could see her complete reflection. In it, she saw the face which did not belong to her.

"Where is Chrona?" she asked the looking glass.

The mirror glimmered and revealed an old castle on a hill. It glimmered again and showed a room. In the center of it sat a fountain, flashing with brilliant light. Then Chrona burst into the room and saw Star Bright's face appear in the water.

"The looking glass is fixed? How can this be?!" the sorceress screamed. She turned into black smoke which poured into the fountain.

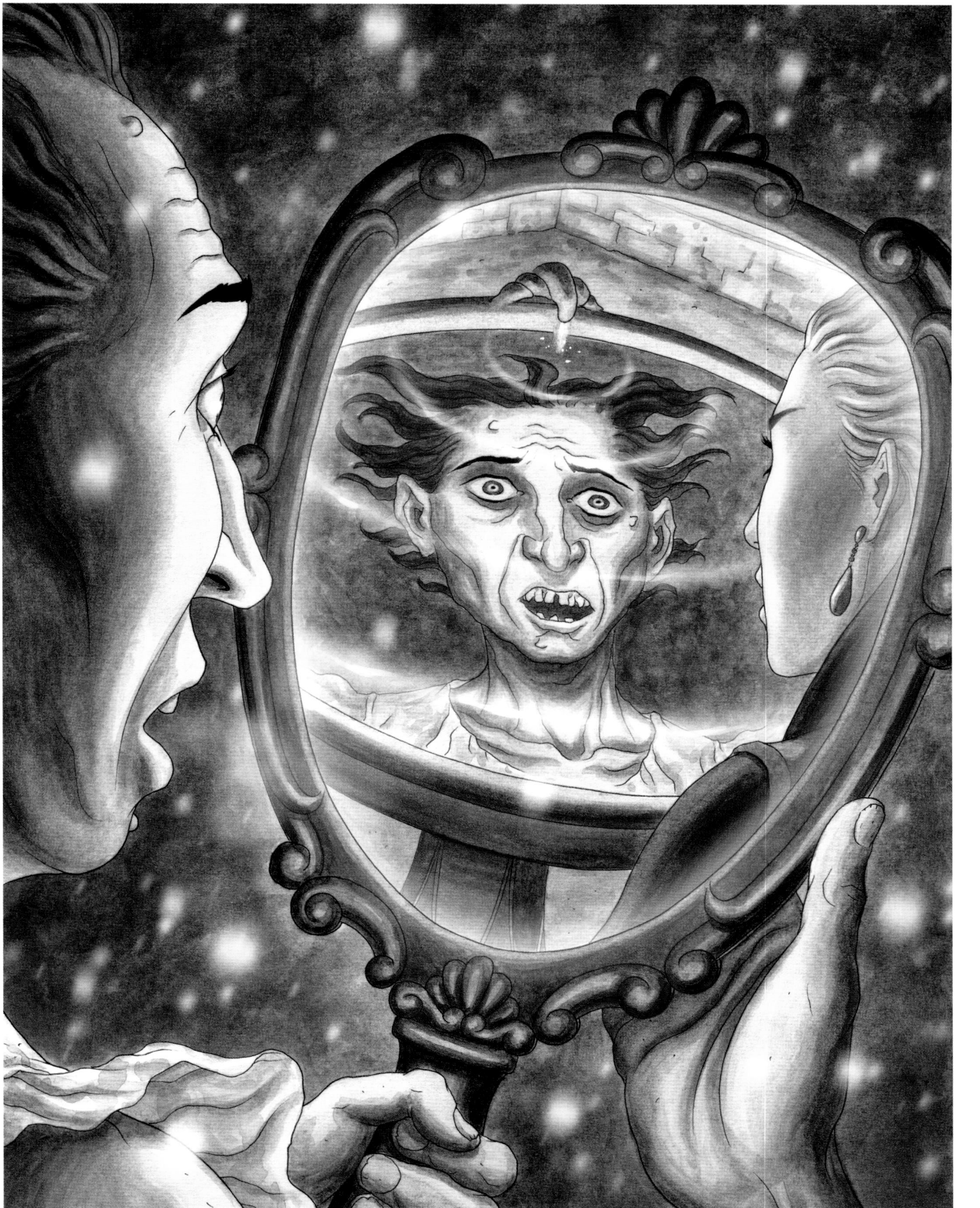

Black smoke shot out of the looking glass. The smoke swirled around the four friends like a dark spirit, formed into a pillar before them, then into a beautiful woman. It was Chrona. She was no longer wearing a simple robe. Instead she wore one of the most beautiful, intricate dresses Star Bright had ever seen; yet it was dark and intimidating as well. It shocked Star Bright to see her body displayed with such exquisite attire and grooming, and a part of her found it appealing.

"Star Bright," hissed Chrona, eyes glaring. "You...fixed the looking glass? How?"

"My friends and I have traveled the world to do so," Star Bright said. "I would like you to return my appearance to me."

"And I would like you to return my looking glass," Chrona said, firing bolts of energy at Star Bright from her hands.

Star Bright instinctively raised the looking glass to protect herself. The bolts hit the mirror and were deflected back to Chrona, striking her to the ground.

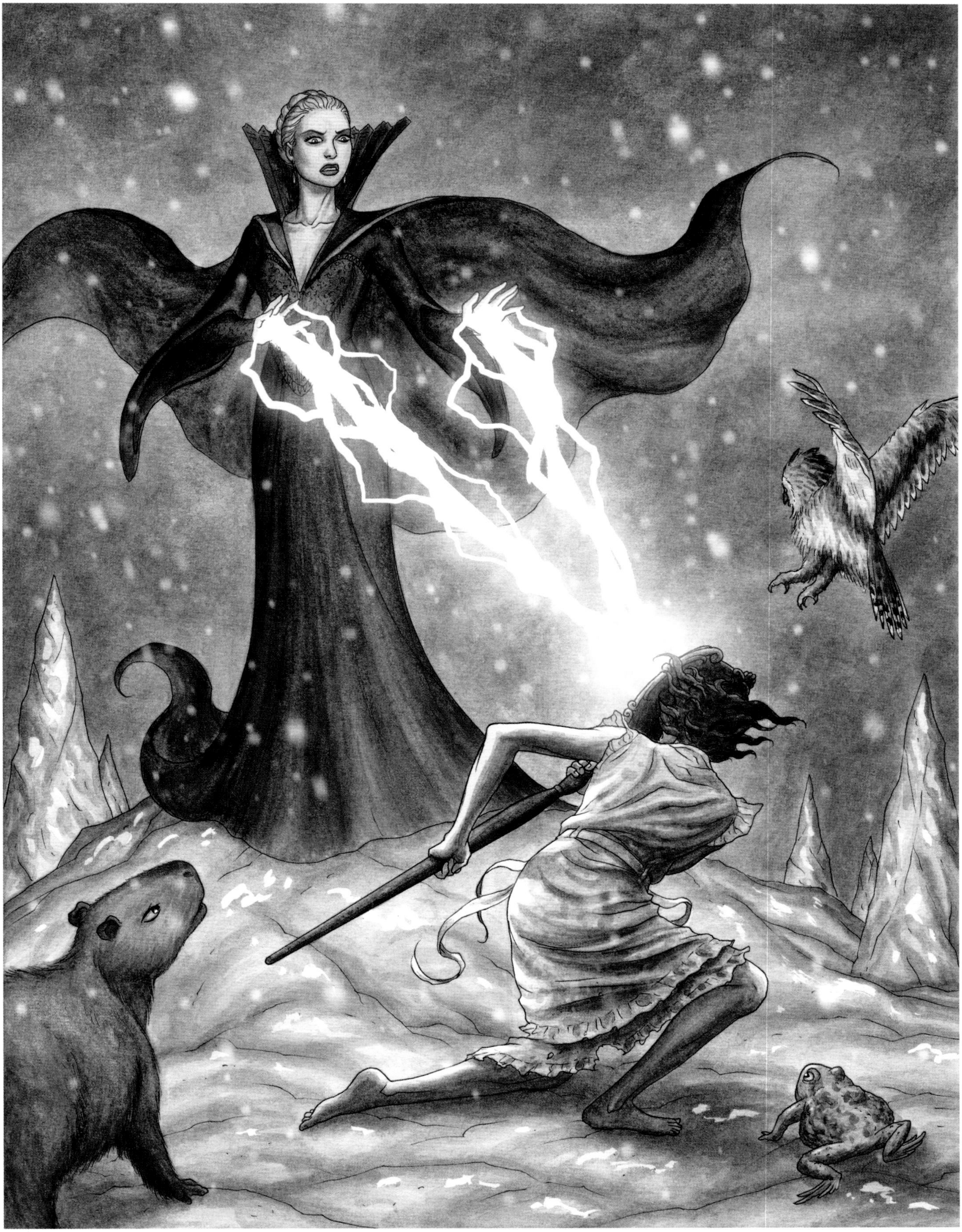

Star Bright held out the looking glass between Chrona and herself, ready to chant.

Chrona raised her hands in defense and said, "Wait! You could die if you switch us back!"

Star Bright paused and narrowed her eyes. "What are you talking about?"

"When my mother stole a maiden's beauty," Chrona began, "something happened that she didn't anticipate; she fell so in love with her appearance that she did nothing but stare at herself for days and days...until she died." She continued, "That's why I destroyed the looking glass. I would have had the same fate. And you would, too."

Star Bright hesitated, thinking about how she had stared at herself for days, as well. But she didn't ponder long. She chanted, "Looking glass, looking glass, spin around; give me the beauty that I have found!"

The looking glass spun and spun, faster and faster, and began to glow. Once again, waves of energy shot out of the looking glass onto Star Bright and Chrona. For a moment, the two were paralyzed, linked by its power.

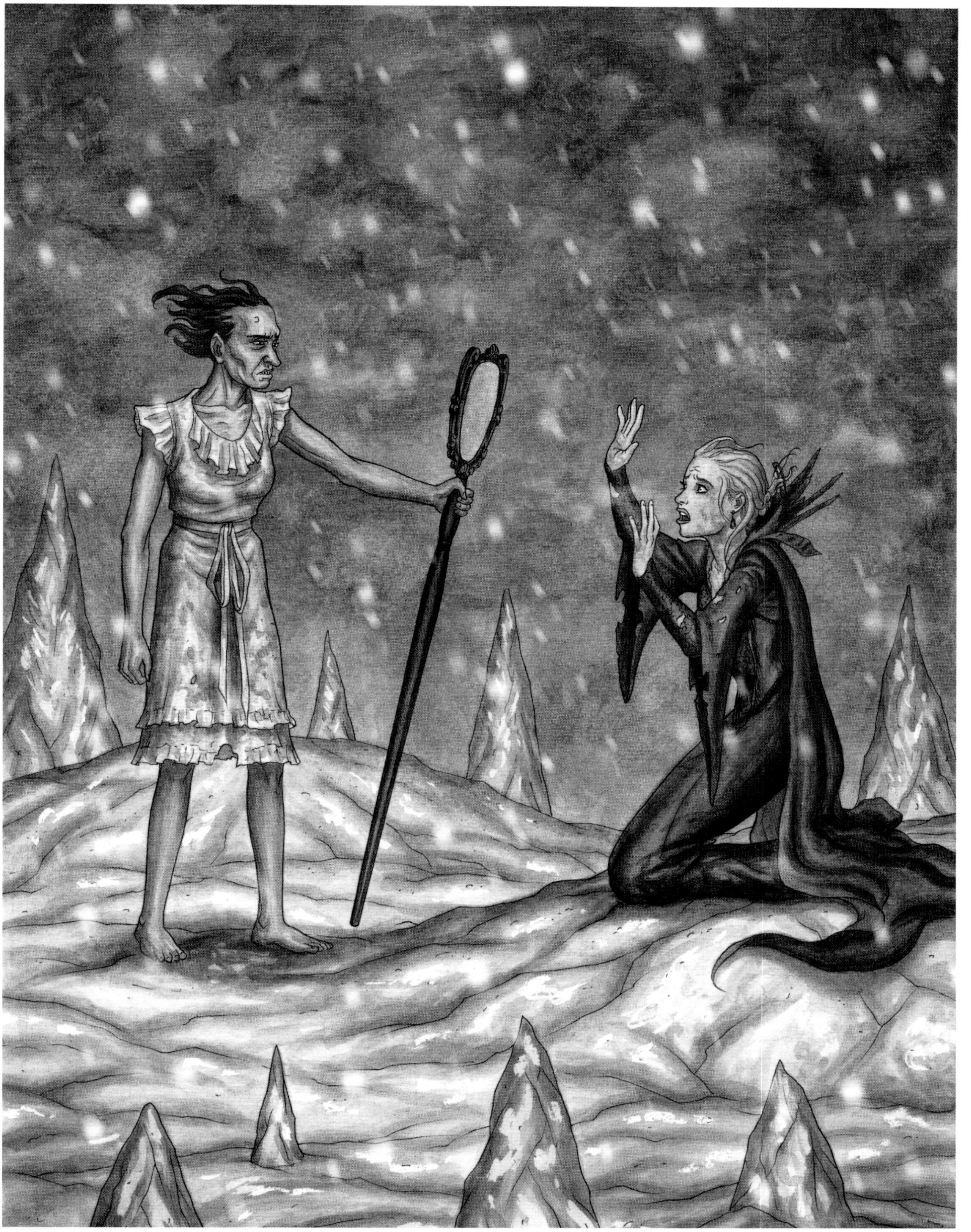

The blinding light died down and Star Bright had her own body once again. Chrona had been returned to her original form as well.

"I'm back to normal!" Star Bright exclaimed. Toad, Owl, and Capybara cheered.

"Nooo!" wailed Chrona, clutching her face. "This can't be! I cannot live with such an ugly face! I must be beautiful!" Suddenly, she lunged for the looking glass, but Toad, Owl, and Capybara pounced on her and held her back.

Star Bright looked in the mirror and saw her beautiful face. For her, everything else in the world turned black. All she wanted to do was stare at her face all day and every day. She admired the shape of her eyes, the slope of her nose, and the curves of her lips.

The animals saw Star Bright frozen, staring at her reflection.

"What is she doing?" Owl asked.

"Oh dear," Toad said.

"I can't hold Chrona back much longer!" Capybara exclaimed.

"Let go of me, you disgusting beasts!" Chrona shouted.

Star Bright looked so happy, gazing into the looking glass—and she was—but then a little thought crept into her mind. She remembered that loving her beauty this much turned her into a monster on the inside. She remembered being horrible to her friends.

Star Bright blinked and looked away from the mirror. Her hair was still tied up from the way Chrona had it, and she loosened it, letting it fall naturally. Then she raised the looking glass to the sky and said to the sorceress, "You asked the looking glass to show you a beautiful maiden no person cares about. But my friends are animals."

Star Bright swung the looking glass down.

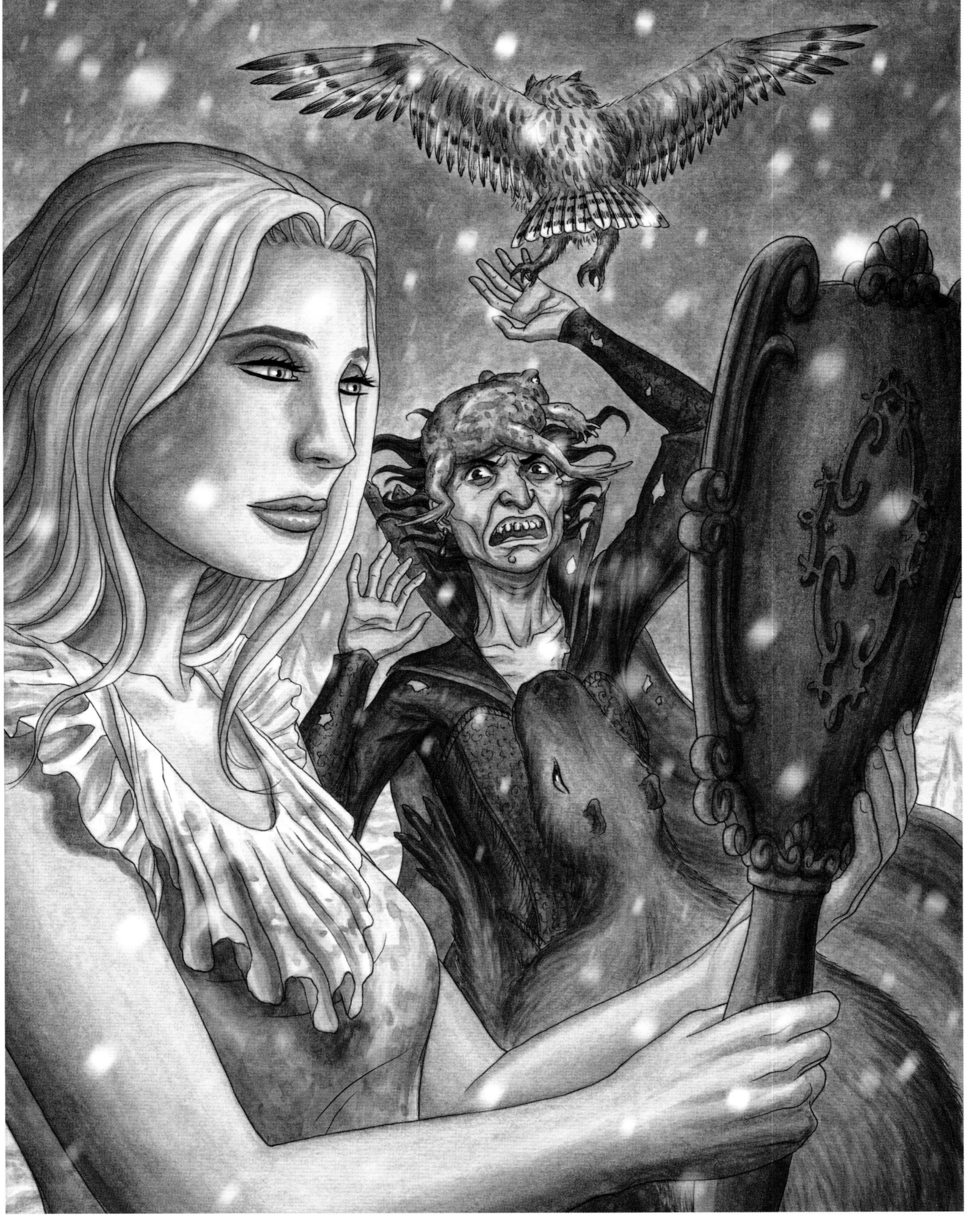

Star Bright struck the looking glass against an icy rock with so much passion that its glass exploded once again—even the frame and staff shattered into pieces. Star Bright, Chrona, and the animals fell on their backs, and the shards were sent flying high into the sky, but this time they did not return to the earth. They shot past the clouds, leaving the atmosphere.

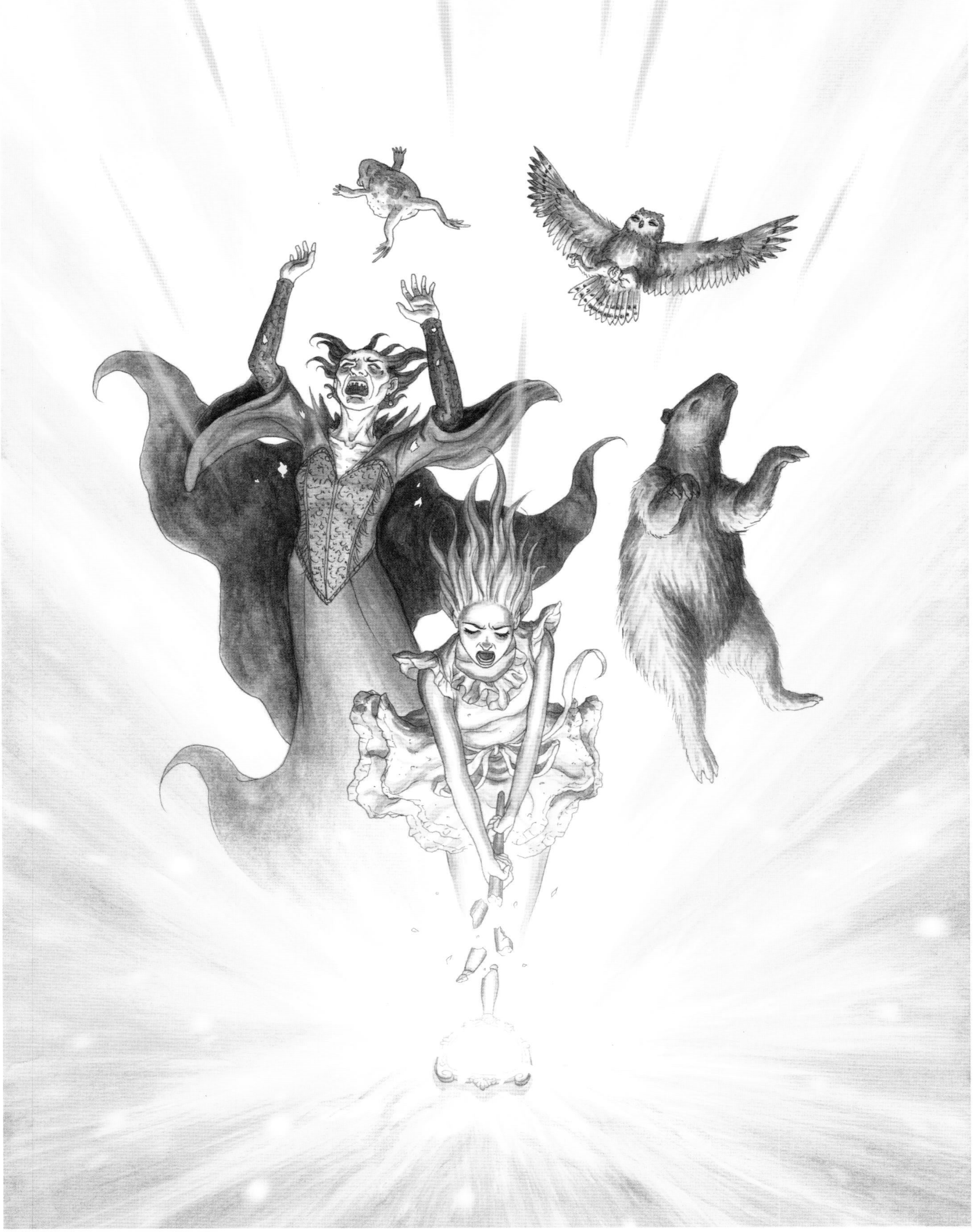

To everyone's surprise, the shards stayed anchored in the sky and joined the stars. The shining shards became known as a constellation, symbolizing the story about an ugly sorceress who tried to steal another woman's beauty. This legend spread to all the people of the world, and the constellation was named after Chrona, who lived the rest of her life hiding in shame.

For a great many years, travelers heard mournful wailing coming from an old castle on a hill.

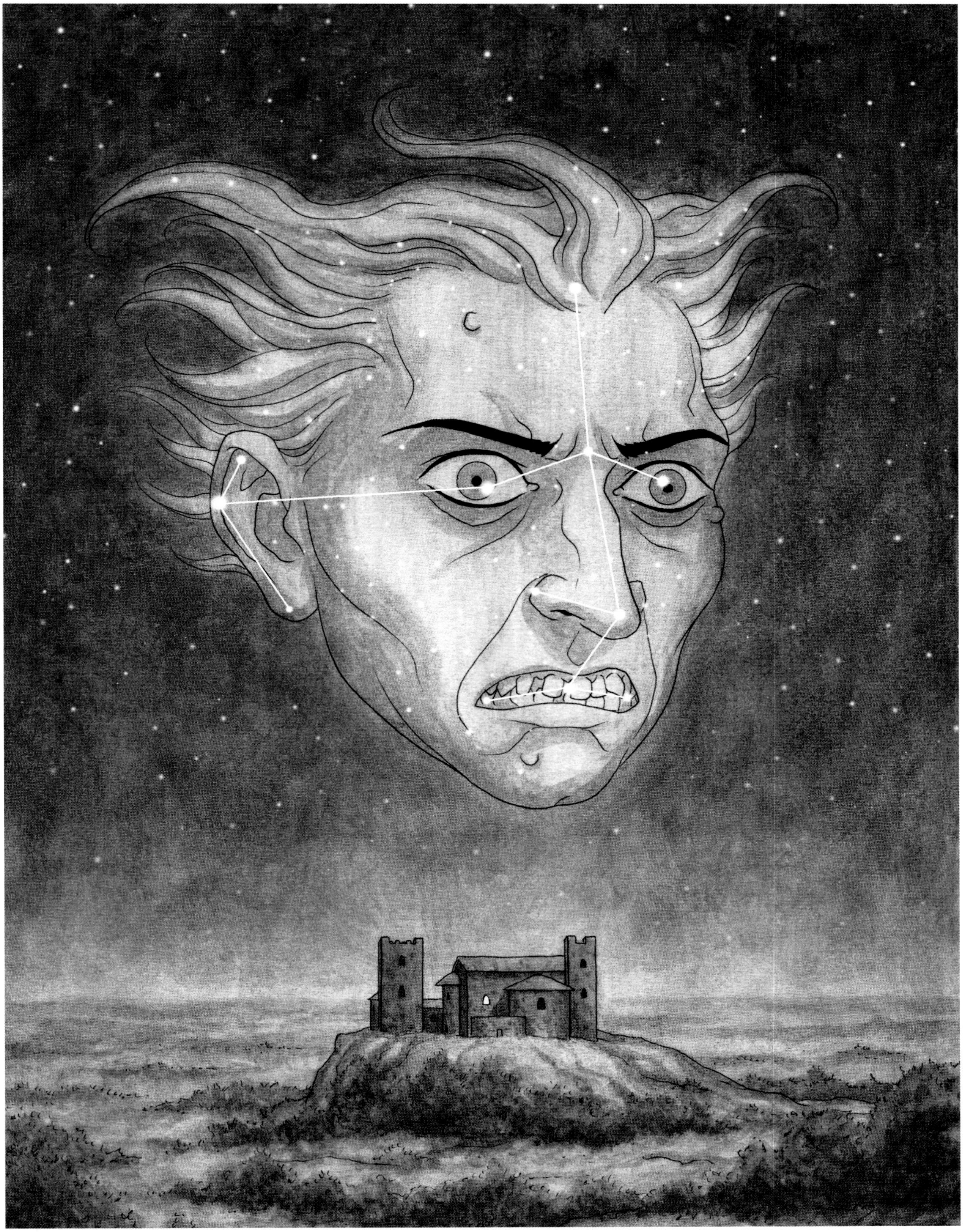

Toad, Owl, Capybara, and Star Bright returned to their home, the wood. After such a long journey, they were very tired. And so they found a comfortable spot below the stars and lay down in the grass to rest their weary bodies and droopy eyelids.

Star Bright was not as prim and elegant as before—nor was she as dirty and unkempt—yet she felt happier than ever.

She looked at her friends and thought about everything they had done for her, and they returned her gaze.

"Dear Toad, dear Owl, dear Capybara," whispered Star Bright, "I love you, too."

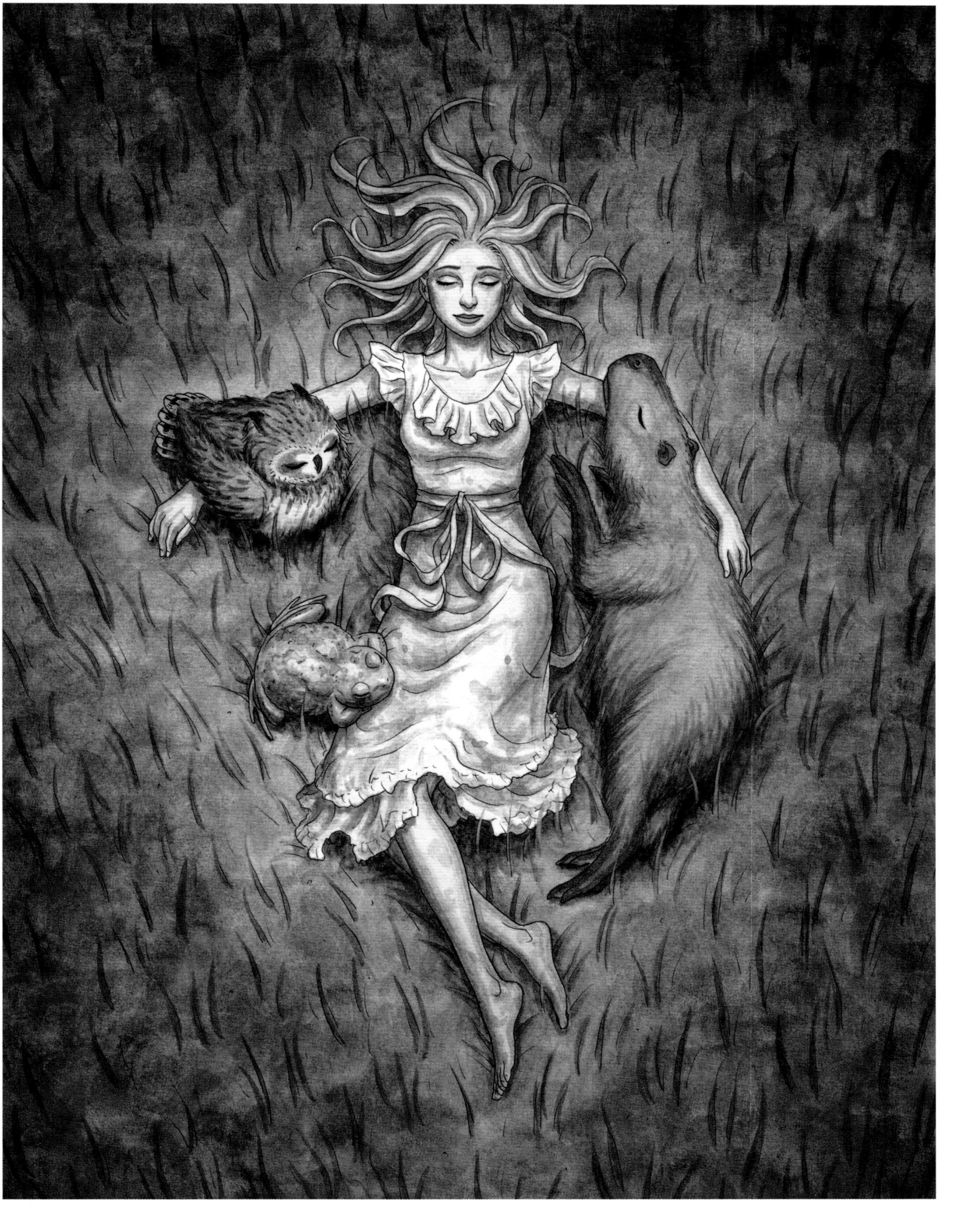

JONATHAN LUNA co-created
THE SWORD, GIRLS, and ULTRA
(all Image Comics) with his brother,
Joshua Luna. His work also includes
the art for SPIDER-WOMAN: ORIGIN
(Marvel Comics), written by Brian
Michael Bendis and Brian Reed.

Jonathan was born in California and
spent most of his childhood overseas,
living on naval bases in Iceland and
Italy. He returned to the United States
in his late teens.

Writing and drawing comics since he
was a child, he graduated from the
Savannah College of Art and Design
with a BFA in Sequential Art.

He currently resides in Northern
Virginia.